REVOLUTIONARY
Paul Revere

REVOLUTIONARY

JOEL J. MILLER

THOMAS NELSON
Since 1798

NASHVILLE DALLAS MEXICO CITY RIO DE JANEIRO

Published in Nashville, Tennessee. Thomas Nelson is a registered trademark of Thomas Nelson, Inc.

Thomas Nelson, Inc., titles may be purchased in bulk for educational, business, fund-raising, or sales promotional use. For information, please e-mail SpecialMarkets@ThomasNelson.com.

Library of Congress Cataloging-in-Publication Data

Miller, Joel, 1975–
    The revolutionary Paul Revere / Joel J. Miller.
        p. cm.
    Includes bibliographical references and index.
    ISBN 978-1-59555-074-3
        1. Revere, Paul, 1735–1818. 2. Massachusetts—History—Revolution, 1775–1783.
3. Statesmen—Massachusetts—Biography. 4. Lexington, Battle of, Lexington, Mass.,
1775. 5. United States—History—Revolution, 1775–1783—Biography.
6. Massachusetts—Biography. I. Title.
    F69.R43M55 2010
    974.4'03092—dc22

                                                            2010002955

Printed in the United States of America

10 11 12 13 RRD 6 5 4 3 2 1

For Megan, Fionn,
and Felicity

What, then, is the American, this new man?

—J. HECTOR ST. JOHN DE CRÈVECOEUR[1]

Paul Revere embodied the new order.

—STEPHEN L. LONGENECKER[2]

Contents

The
REVOLUTIONARY
Paul Revere

Prologue

Paul Revere sat down at his desk. He readied a quill, opened an ink bottle, and spread several sheets of paper before him. He was an old man now, gray-haired and wrinkled, but his eyes were bright. Those brilliant brown gems gleamed as intensely as they did when he was young. Back then his hair was dark enough to match, worn long, and tied back in a queue. Now it was cut short and hung loose about his collar. Young or old, he was always a stocky man, thick in the chest and shoulders, his rugged hands used to long days firing furnaces, hammering billets of silver, and wielding cold chisels and etching needles. Now those sturdy and calloused fingers took up his pen.

He wrote to Rev. Jeremy Belknap, a local minister, historian, and the secretary of the Massachusetts Historical Society. "Dear Sir," he started, each stroke and cross of his quill making a light scratching sound on the surface of the paper. "Having a little leisure, I wish to fullfill my promise, of giving you some facts, and Anecdotes, prior to the Battle of Lexington, which I do not remember to have seen in any history of the American Revolution."[1] Belknap and his associates at the society desired to gather and preserve as many historical records as possible. Revere's story fit the bill perfectly.

It was now 1797, more than two decades after those events, and they were still firebrand fresh in his mind, such as the time when he rode to New York, freighted with news about the Boston Tea Party, or to Philadelphia with copies of the Suffolk Resolves tucked in his leather saddlebags. Others were fresher still.

He wrote about the time when he and several other artisans and mechanics formed a spy ring "for the purpose of watching the Movements of the British Soldiers, and gaining every intelegence of the movements of the Tories." He told Belknap how they would take turns, "two and two, to Watch the Soldiers, By patroling the Streets all night." Bad luck for the patriots; they weren't the only spies. Revere told Belknap about a traitor who exposed all their secrets to the British general and royal governor, Thomas Gage.

Revere's pen swept across the page, describing one

scene after another (all with the idiosyncratic spelling and punctuation common to the time). Central to the whole story was the night of 18 April 1775. As he penned it, redcoats mustered, and Paul's friend, the patriot leader Joseph Warren "beged that I would imediately Set off for Lexington, where Messrs. Hancock and Adams were, and that it was thought they were the objets."

He wrote about how he set a signal in North Church steeple, rowed across the Charles River, borrowed a horse, and charged across Charlestown Neck toward Lexington; how he ran into a British patrol, evaded capture, and "alarmed almost every House, till I got to Lexington," where he alerted John Hancock and Samuel Adams to the approaching danger.

He told about how he met up with one rider, then another, and how the three of them set off to spread the alarm to Concord, a town just up the road, where colonists kept a vast store of gunpowder and arms.

Paul never made it. As he told Belknap, a redcoat patrol ambushed them. The patrol nabbed Revere, and an officer "clapped his pistol to my head, called me by name, and told me he . . . would blow my brains out." After some questioning, Paul and the soldiers heard a volley fired, coming from Lexington. It spooked the redcoats. The militia was out. The soldiers took Paul's horse, let him go, and bolted away into the dark. The moon threw a pale light on the wet ground, and Revere was able to make his way by its cast. He stumbled through the headstones of a graveyard and some pastures until he came again into Lexington.

After Paul's arrival, Adams and Hancock decided to leave Lexington for Woburn, a nearby village, far enough away from the imminent trouble. Paul joined them, saw that they arrived safely, and then made his way back to Lexington in the early morning hours. Once back, he walked toward Buckman Tavern and "a Man on a full gallop . . . told us the Troops were coming up the Rocks." Another rider confirmed it. The bristling tips of British gun barrels would pierce the horizon in any minute. The militiamen readied themselves. The fight was upon them.

Paul's account was exactly what Belknap wanted to hear and would undoubtedly make a superb addition to the society's collection.

But there was so much more to the story.

CHAPTER I

Arrivals

*In which the forebears of our hero trade the
trials and hardships of the Old World for the
uncertainties and hopes of the New, starting
our story rolling in the boisterous town of
Boston, in the British colony of Massachusetts.*

This land grows weary of its inhabitants." That's what
John Winthrop thought of his home.[1] England was
too small, geographically, theologically, politically, and
economically. He couldn't stand the cramp, and the feeling
was mutual: England couldn't stand him. Winthrop was
a Puritan and ran afoul of the Act of Uniformity, which
outlawed doctrinal squabbles (something at which the
Puritans excelled) in the Anglican Church.

It came to this: Winthrop, a onetime government law-
yer, needed new digs, preferably where he could structure

1

a little government of his own. So in 1630 he gained control of the Massachusetts Bay Company and led a pack of Puritans to America. Picture Moses leaving Egypt with the children of Israel, except in this case the promised land *was* the wilderness.

The plan was to settle in Salem. Some Pilgrims were already there, and Winthrop figured they could farm alongside. But that plan was hatched several thousand miles away, and when Winthrop and company actually arrived, they realized that clearing the dense woodland was too big a chore. They could hunt the game-thick forest, but they were largely inexperienced, and Winthrop was a klutz with a gun. As a young man, he gave up hunting because "I have gotten . . . nothing at all towards my cost and labor," a roundabout way of admitting that he was a lousy shot.[2] So, down with Salem.

After further scouting the New England coast, Winthrop decided on the peninsula of Trimountain, as the earliest English settlers first called Boston.[3] It had ample room at seven hundred square acres, good drinking water, and breathtaking landscape. The best feature? The mile-long muddy finger that gripped the mainland. Boston Neck doesn't exist today as it did then. In the seventeenth century, before the hills were leveled into the bay to expand the land mass, the slender sinew was narrow enough to keep enemies out (or inhabitants bottled in, as the British army would later discover).[4]

The Puritans had their base of operation; now they had to operate. England might have grown weary of its inhabitants, but fledgling colonies needed to create businesses profitable enough to survive in their new homes and enrich underwriters and benefactors in their old. Fattening British purses was a colony's reason for existence—so much so that colonies were often called "plantations."[5] Production was the whole point.

Virginia had tobacco.

New York had furs.

And Boston had the "sacred cod."[6]

It's an apt adjective. The fish is one of the earliest Christian symbols, so it makes a providential sort of sense that Winthrop and his Puritans bettered themselves through the burgeoning industry. He didn't have the foresight to keep up his hunting practice as a lad, but he was smart enough to bring shipbuilders with him to the New World. As one observation had it, "[T]he Puritans took to sea with such vigor that . . . their commerce smelled as strongly of fish as their theology did of brimstone."[7] By 1640, Massachusetts exported three hundred thousand dried and salted cod, the very foundation for Boston's future wealth and status.[8]

By the time Paul Revere's father, Apollos Rivoire, hit shore in 1716, the settlement had grown from a bedraggled band barely fit to occupy the dirt under their feet to a bustling and prosperous seaside city of nearly fifteen thousand inhabitants, bursting with as many opportunities as people. No mistaking it: Boston was an unweary place.

English Puritans were not alone in the world. A like-minded group, the Huguenots, lived in the predominantly Catholic France. But just as England wearied of its inhabitants, France tired of its Huguenots—to the point of persecution. Fearing trouble, Isaac Rivoire baptized newborn son Apollos in secret in 1702 because the law forbade Protestant rites.

Huguenots dodged trouble in three ways; they phonied up an allegiance to Rome, kept a low profile, or took off. Isaac opted for one of the first two. He owned land near the wine-rich region of Bordeaux and remained there the rest of his life. But he chose option three for Apollos. Sending the boy away must have been hard, though not as difficult as watching authorities seize the child should they suspect Isaac of teaching him Protestant doctrines. So in November 1715, thirteen-year-old Apollos boarded a boat for the English Channel Island of Guernsey. His uncle Simon previously fled there and now arranged for Apollos's passage from Guernsey to Boston.[9]

If young Apollos's trip was typical, then the journey was probably rough. Food stores, often insufficient, just as often went bad. Stormy winter waves endangered anyone above decks. Most passengers trekked it below in the ill-lit, damp interior, the ship throbbing and undulating with the nauseating swell of the sea. Cramped quarters, poor food, and stale air meant that voyagers often took sick. Days and weeks passed, and the voyage seemed interminable.

Then land. Lumpen masses rose from the sea. Hazy coastline sharpened and firmed against the horizon. Smells of earth and vegetation blew from shore as the ship approached.

Threading narrow Nantasket Channel, the vessel glided past Castle Island on the right. On the left, Governour's Island and then little Bird Island. Steering clear of the shallow Dorchester Flats, the ship washed into a welcoming wharf and disgorged its cargo as excited passengers bounded ashore. All but Apollos, whose family indentured the boy to pay for his apprenticeship to goldsmith John Coney. Apollos could no more do as he pleased than could one of the slaves attending the brocaded merchants by the docks.

Indenture ensured long-term care and safety. Apprentices were guaranteed humane treatment, room, board, and education. But for this moment, while he waited for the captain to transfer him to his new master, Apollos was also guaranteed the dehumanized status of a living, breathing transaction waiting for paperwork and fulfillment.

View of Boston's harbors.
Library of Congress.

Commerce was everything. Boston's fortunes were built on cod, but trade follows trade. For that John Winthrop could have hardly picked a better spot. Boston was well sheltered and closer to England than any other American port. The shoreline sprouted an ever-growing tangle of wharves, docks, and shipyards, all sprawling over the water's edge as if the peninsula were pulsing and alive.

Trimountain was nothing like the calm, rolling hills of Bordeaux. Likely both anxious and fearful, Apollos took in the display around him. The skyline jagged in its hectic array of rooflines, bristling with church steeples and glinting weather vanes. Wharves spiked with ship masts. Merchants, sailors, and artisans scurrying along wooden planks and muddy streets, in and out of warehouses, counting houses, shops, inns, taverns, and coffeehouses, hasty with errands and missions. Shipwrights and joiners bending to their tasks, maintaining the fleets of vessels that brought textiles from England, sugar from the Caribbean, wine from the Canaries, tea from Holland, and slaves from Africa. Within earshot there were the clink-clinking of hammers, the ringing and clanging of bells, the haggling of shopkeeps, the shouting of tradesmen, the cursing of seamen, the barking of seals, the cawing of gulls. Maritime smells suffused the air: salty breezes, hot tar, wood smoke, breweries, rum distilleries, soap boilers, whaleworks, and of course, fish, particularly cod—caked with salt and drying in the sun, ready to make its way back to the ports and markets of England and Europe, possibly even Rochelle, the port from which Apollos forever departed his home only months before.[10]

A long shot from the serene vineyards of home—stretching before him now was the turbulent preurban tussle of Boston and the vast expanse of America.

CHAPTER 2

Ascent

*In which the father of our hero, Apollos Rivoire,
comes into his own, and changes the family name
before buying his freedom, marrying a good
Yankee girl of hardy stock, and then
bringing little Paul into a world
beset by economic troubles.*

For all the freshness and novelty of America, some things didn't change. As apprentice and master, Apollos and Coney commenced a relationship unaltered since the Middle Ages. Apollos had to learn, serve, submit, and not embarrass or harm Coney by thieving, whoring, gambling, or boozing. He was, as the standard contract language had it, to "behave himself as a faithful apprentice ought." Meanwhile, Coney's job was to provide "sufficient meat, drink, apparel, lodging and washing befitting an apprentice" and to "use the utmost of his endeavor" to teach his "trade or mystery."[1]

It was a lucky stroke for Apollos that New England boasted some of the finest goldsmiths in the colonies, and Coney was one of the best. There were around five hundred working in America then, some good, some bad. Apollos might have been apprenticed to a hack and been degraded day and night. Benjamin Franklin, just a few years Apollos's junior, was indentured to his abusive brother, a Boston printer. Ben split for Philadelphia rather than buckle under. Many apprentices beat town, just as many masters beat the stragglers into submission. Things weren't so bad for Apollos.

Coney showed Apollos the tools and techniques of the trade: how to melt silver coinage and recast it as salver, tankard, or bowl; how to beat an ingot of silver into a large sheet; how to raise a disc of flattened silver into a teapot; how to engrave everything from porringers to printing plates.

Apollos spoke no English but picked up his new tongue with his craft. He proved a quick study, capable, industrious, and worked hard to apply himself. In time he turned an ample income, enough by 1729 to purchase a copy of *The Life of the Very Reverend and Learned Cotton Mather*, evidence of decent finances, religious devotion, and adequate command of the language. So thoroughly anglicized was Apollos by this point that he called himself "Paul" and changed his last name "Rivoire" to "Revere." His son, our story's Paul Revere, said he made the switch because "the Bumpkins pronounce it easier."[2] At least he hadn't lost that native French charm. To avoid confusion I'll use the old name, but the change is significant. While some things remained the same continent to continent, other things changed dramatically. Out of the persecutions and struggles of the Old World, Apollos emerged a new man in a New World, so self-possessed he rechristened himself with a name of his own invention.[3]

Apollos never finished his apprenticeship under Coney. In 1722, the old man died. Coney's widow could now sell his indenture, and with the death of her husband, she might well need the cash. Facing several additional years of uncertain servitude, Apollos pulled together the funds and bought his own contract.

Freedom.

No longer the captive boy on the dock, he could now do as he pleased.[4]

Deborah Hitchborn, as it happened, pleased him right down to the ground. Apprentices took up with the boss's daughters often enough, and Coney had a handful within easy reach. But convenience isn't everything, and Apollos cast his gaze in a different direction. Deborah lived next door.

Puritans were supposed to hold two competing values in tension: "diligence in worldly business, and yet deadness to the world." That's from the pen of Puritan divine John Cotton.[5] The Hitchborn family was expert in the former even if members sometimes flagged in the latter. Thomas, the paterfamilias, built and repaired ships, operated a tavern, and owned Hitchborn Wharf, a mansion, and several other properties. He was not unique. Since hitting the New England dirt, succeeding generations of Hitchborns and their in-laws commonly hiked further up the ladder of success and status. Even the rowdy ones like Thomas Dexter, an infamous scofflaw whose only known hobbies were cheating Indians and offending magistrates, made their ascent rung by rung.[6]

Coney's neighbor Deborah saw Apollos trying the same hand-over-fist climb. Now he was finally in business for himself. She could do worse for a husband. The couple married 19 June 1729, when he was twenty-seven and she was twenty-five.[7]

The newlyweds kept climbing. Within a year of marrying, they announced in *The Weekly News Letter* their move "from Capt Pitt's, at the Town Dock, to the North End over against Col Hutchinson's."[8]

Their new neighbor, the Colonel, was one of Boston's leading citizens, a merchant who weathered the hazardous waves of oceangoing commerce and came out ahead more times than not. Pilasters and a cupola adorned his brickwork manse. Fenced and girt with gardens, the estate counted fruit trees and coach houses among its rare features.[9]

The Reveres moved next door with big hopes. The North End was a cramped and cockeyed place where wealthy merchants and common artisans shared scarce space, and proximity promised business. It was handy for a goldsmith to have wealthy merchants in the neighborhood; they were always needing salvers and tea sets. The Reveres encountered the Hutchinsons on the street and saw them at church, the New Brick Church, commonly called the Cockerel after its rooster-shaped brass weather vane.[10] Apollos would soon count the Colonel and his rising-star son, Thomas Hutchinson, as customers.

Financial advantage was no doubt on Apollos's mind. The Puritan ethic might have made wealth more likely— hard work never hurt—but it guaranteed nothing. Boston suffered from several economic crises. Smallpox hit in the twenties, and deaths tallied almost two thousand, wiping out as much as an eighth of the total population.[11] Traders avoided the wharves. Farmers avoided the markets. The Revere family felt the financial impact long after the birth of Paul's eldest sibling. Deborah, named for her mother, arrived in 1732. Apollos had enough money to muster his *Mather* in '29, but there was less jingle in the purse now, and his family was growing.

As Boston recouped from those shocks, Parliament leveled another. The Molasses Act of 1733 slowed the spigot of cheap French molasses to American distillers. Pity more than poor tipplers. Rum was big business, so that blow was bad enough, but industries connected to the trade staggered as well. Orders for new ships fell by half. Cuts in the fishing trade—the cornerstone of Boston's economy—were even more dramatic. Sailors, carpenters, rope makers, and others felt the bruise and, as one writer put the additional misfortune, "did not even have the consolation of cheap rum in which to drown their sorrows."[12]

Apollos and Deborah's second child, our Paul Revere, arrived a year later, in December 1734, on the twenty-first day of the month, and the family finances suffered throughout his early years.

The Reveres knew from the Bible that the love of money was the root of all evil. They also knew that the lack of it wasn't much better. English trade laws rerouted gold and silver back to England, where it stayed. Enough of the coinage that colonists kept ended up as spoons, bowls, and tankards that they were constantly short on specie. Following philosopher David Hume's comparison of money in an economy to oil in a wheel-housing, the Massachusetts economy was grinding along with a fair share of bumps and knocks.[13] Between 1736 and 1738 Apollos found himself strapped and dragged into court three times for debts he couldn't pay.[14]

Without hard cash, colonists had to get creative. They printed paper money. Apollos's old master was one of the colony's first engravers and printers of the stuff. But paper currency had drawbacks, the worst of which was that it never seemed to be worth as much one day as it was the day before.

Merchants and shop owners turned to barter. Grain, gunpowder, and salt cod replaced pounds, shillings, and doubloons. Oats for hymnbooks and Bibles. Molasses for guns and blankets. Leading merchant Thomas Hancock kept detailed records. Biographer Harlow Giles Unger tells of one particular trade: a tailor purchased tea, paper, and gloves from Hancock in exchange for, among other things, two pairs of britches for Hancock's young nephew John.[15]

Another stopgap combined the best of both paper money and barter. The former was issued as a loan based on the value of mortgaged properties. Payment was accepted in kind—flax, iron, anything marketable.[16] The "land bank" scheme provided liquid currency to a thirsty economy, but it also stoked fears among some, including Paul Revere's neighbor Thomas Hutchinson.

The illustrious Thomas Hutchinson.
New York Public Library.

While many around him lost their shirts as fast as their footing, Hutchinson was making great strides and was soon to replace his father, the Colonel, in local prestige. He had a thin, boyishly handsome face, oversized eyes and nose over full lips and a retreating, lightly dimpled chin—all of it framed in the dark-gray curls of his peruke. His public image welcomed characterizations as conservative, prudent, honorable, popular. The town elected him selectman in 1737. He then picked up a seat in the lower house of the Bay Colony legislature, known as the General Court.

Hutchinson was not alone in considering the land bank scheme unstable and injurious to his interests. Merchants and aristocrats opposed it. They worried about inflation and the loss of their fortunes, so they lobbied Parliament. The authorities dropped the hammer, and several people were ruined in the fallout, including the father of Samuel Adams, a leading organizer in Boston politics. To Hutchinson's later chagrin, Adams, then a student at Harvard, never forgot.[17]

CHAPTER 3

Moxie

In which our hero grows up, learns
his ABCs along with his father's trade
of goldsmithing, shows self-determination,
and gets a whupping for going to church—
all before tragedy strikes the family.

When Paul was nine, the family moved to a house at the head of Clark's Wharf on Fish Street. It was the same neighborhood as their previous digs, just closer to the water's edge. Their landlord, Dr. John Clark, had tradesmen and sea captains for tenants.[1]

Water hemmed Boston, and that's where the real action happened. Boats coming and going, cargo offloaded one ship, freight hoisted upon another, exotic sights, sounds, and more. Men bent their backs all along the wharves, making rope and boiling tar, busying themselves distilling rum, drying fish, and forging steel. A boy could have any number of adventures in the thick of it all.

In the hot months, Revere and pals like Josiah Flagg would have enjoyed swimming. North Battery was a military installment just a few blocks from Revere's home. Later in life Paul engraved a picture depicting its solemn blockwork fortifications, a wind-blown Union Jack, boats aprowl in the bay, and a large ship docked behind the palisades. And a bonus: in the lower left-hand corner he added three boys leaping into the water. Curious because the depiction was engraved for an official military certificate. And yet there it is, a frivolous detail thrown in for fun, a likely glimpse into the boyhood of Paul Revere.[2]

And then school. Bostonians valued education, as did colonists from most of the Puritan-settled areas. Reading assignments, memory work, and stern teachers—who meted out punishment as quickly as more lessons—were the norm. No one should, as one law on the Massachusetts books put it, "suffer so much barbarism in any of their families as not to endeavor to teach by themselves or others, their children and apprentices so much learning as may enable them perfectly to read the English tongue and knowledge of the Capital laws."[3] Violators found themselves twenty shillings lighter per infraction.

Public schools were founded in Massachusetts to aid the endeavor, and Boston had at least five.[4] There were two basic tracks for students. The first was for children who were highborn or destined for the ministry. They attended the Latin schools. The others were for the poor or those destined for the trades. They attended the writing schools. The former would study the classics and learn foreign languages—Latin, Hebrew, and Greek—before moving on to an institution such as Harvard or Yale. The latter would be taught the basics of math and reading and would end formal education by their early teens so they could start their apprenticeships. Revere attended North Writing School.

Along with academic schooling, the law mandated that Paul and his siblings be schooled in the faith.[5] The Westminster Shorter Catechism was designed specifically for children. Several editions of the ubiquitous *New England Primer*—including the one current when Paul was in school —featured the catechism as well as other items of religious significance, such as prayers. Some became commonplace:

Now I lay me down to take my sleep
I pray the Lord my soul to keep,
If I should die before I wake,
I pray the Lord my soul to take.

Others did not, though they contained sentiments shared by Paul's Puritan forebears, neighbors, and later descendants:

Lord if thou lengthen out my days
Then let my heart so fixed be

That I may lengthen out thy praise
And never turn aside from thee.[6]

Whatever the tool, method, or content, it is very likely that religious instruction was featured in the Revere household—especially considering father Apollos's devotion.

Once he'd mastered all there was to know in the world (or at least enough for the son of an artisan) Paul would have ceased formal schooling, strapped on a leather apron, and commenced apprenticeship with his dad, probably around age twelve or thirteen. Perhaps happy to be free of the endless ciphers and rote memorization, maybe anticipating the thrills of learning the mysteries of his father's craft, Paul felt his initial excitement tempered by the menial and lackluster nature of his first tasks in the silver shop, tidying things up, tending the fires, observing. But as he applied himself, he went deeper into the trade. Eventually he learned to beat a billet of silver flat as a board, cast cup handles and other shapes from molten silver, manage the mercurial magic of silver solder, and engrave the final product with restrained and delicate designs. Soon he could smith a salver and turn a tankard with the best of them.

The majority of the big work, the teapots and salvers, was done in the Queen Anne style, characterized by simplicity and elegance. Cream pots and other vessels Paul later made in this style reflect what he learned in his father's shop: bulbous pyriform bodies and sweeping, elegant handles with simple adornment.

From his father, Paul would have become keen to the beauty of silver. As one writer captures its lure, "The evanescence of the surface allows silver objects to merge with their surroundings, absorbing the colors around them and, by glints of reflection, disguising form and focusing attention instead on constantly changing surfaces."[7] This is especially true of more elaborately decorated work of the rococo style with which Paul soon experimented. Though it was in metal of a different sort—the bronze of church bells—that Paul's maturity first really shows.

Christ Church, also known as the North Church, built on the slope of Copp's Hill, was an Anglican congregation that had an elaborate and impressive bell system. At fifteen, Revere decided to give them a ring.

This must have been a bit of a problem for Paul's dad. Apollos favored the Puritan approach to Christianity. He tithed four shillings a week to his Puritan congregation, the Cockerel, which was substantial compared to the tithing of wealthier men. Now here was Paul, flirting around the edges of an Anglican assembly. Recall from the earlier story of John Winthrop that Puritans and Anglicans didn't play well together. They fought wars over their varying interpretations of the faith. At least Paul wasn't attending sermons there. He was only ringing the bells. And that for a little money. Dad put his cautions on hold.

Paul and friends created an official bellringers' guild.

There were eight boys in all, one for each bell, including Josiah Flagg, John Dyer, and Joseph Snelling. Together, they signed a solemn pact:

> We the Subscribers Do agree To the Following Articles Viz
>
> That if we Can have Liberty From the wardens of Doctor Cuttler's church, we will Attend there once a week on Evenings to ring the Bells for two hours Each time from the date hereof For one year.
>
> That we will Choose a Moderator Every three Months whose Business Shall be To give out the Charges and other Business as Shall be Agreed by a Majority of Voices then Present.
>
> That none shall be admitted a Member of the Society without Unanimous Vote of the Members then Present and that No member Shall begg Money of any Person In the Tower on Penalty of being Excluded the Society, and that we will Attend To Ring at any Time when the Wardens of the Church Aforesaid shall desire it on Penalty of Paying three Shillings for the good of the Society. . . .

After agreeing that "all Differences" were "To be decided By a Majority of Voices," the boys plied the pen. Paul's signature appears second down with an elaborate flourish of scrollwork, right above Flagg's.[8] Historian David Hackett Fischer points to the document as evidence of Paul's budding value system. Self-government, free asso-

ciation, majority will, private responsibility, public duty—
they're all there ready to uncurl and grow.[9]

But Revere had his problems with houses of worship,
too, and one that wasn't so easy for his father to excuse.

It's not every boy who gets a thumping for going to church.
Paul was special.

When he was about fifteen years old, the young Revere
started sneaking away from the Cockerel to listen to Rev.
Jonathan Mayhew, a controversial pastor who manned
one of the most radical pulpits in town, West Church
on Lynde Street. It's not surprising that Revere would be
attracted to Mayhew's preaching. His approach was as
winsome as it was provocative. "He addressed both the
old and the young," writes one of his biographers, "with
peculiar force and appropriateness, and seized every occasion for . . . making religious impressions on the minds of
his people. . . ."[10]

This did not sit well at all with the elder Revere. Ringing
bells for the Anglicans was bad enough. But now Paul was
sneaking away from the family church to catch Mayhew's
preaching? His views were so unorthodox that he hadn't
even joined the local association of Congregational ministers and wouldn't have been welcomed if he had. It pushed
Pop right over the edge.

Some suggest that Mayhew's politics were the problem, and at first blush this might seem true. Around the
same time Paul began attending, Mayhew preached "A

Discourse Concerning Unlimited Submission and Non-Resistance to the Higher Powers," delivered on the anniversary of Charles I's 1649 execution at the hands of Oliver Cromwell. The "divine right of kings" and the "doctrine of nonresistance," he said, are "altogether as fabulous and chimerical as . . . any of the most absurd reveries of ancient or modern visionaries."[11] Mayhew's political views stemmed from the same Calvinist tradition that spawned a wide literature on rights, liberties, and civil disobedience. Though John Calvin opposed rebellion, his Huguenot and Puritan heirs in the Old World (and later in the New) defended it.[12] And these arguments and exhortations flowed easily from pens and pulpits throughout New England.[13] Something else was bothering Apollos.

Mayhew graduated from Harvard and was ordained in

Paul Revere's engraving of the turbulent Rev. Jonathan Mayhew.
New York Public Library.

1747. Enthusiastic and progressive, he was a forerunner to what Thomas Paine later tagged the Age of Reason. Reacting in part to the heavy emotionalism of the Great Awakening, which started in the 1730s, Mayhew became a pioneer for a much more rationalistic, Enlightenment-infused religion, one that valued reason above revelation and philosophy over faith. He seemed to discount original sin, deny total depravity, even reject the trinitarian view of God.[14]

Because most New England churches governed themselves congregation by congregation, there was no hierarchy to contain doctrinal error or police heresy. The end result was a fracturing of the faith in Boston and the surrounding areas that could not be checked, and the fault lines already showed. So when young Revere sneaked sermons at Mayhew's, he was doing something much more unnerving to a pious conservative parent than listening to an antigovernment screed. He was lending ear to a heretic. Politics was politics, but questions of religion had eternal consequences.

Apollos implored his son to quit Mayhew's church, but Paul insisted. The argument grew intense. Finally earnest father struck disobedient son.[15]

The story ends anticlimactically, and nothing else is really known after the fight. Paul apparently came around. He returned to the family church, though he did personally befriend Mayhew—whose proximity to the family only increased after he married the daughter of Revere's landlord[16]—and remained an admirer after Mayhew died more than a dozen years later.

Apollos never saw the friendship endure. He died in July 1754.

That sad summer Paul Revere laid his father to rest— the man who had reared him, taught him, even contested for his soul—in the Granary burial ground. Now, not even twenty years old, Paul was responsible for a sizable family. There were his grieving mother, Deborah; older sister, Deborah; younger brothers, Thomas and John; and three younger sisters, Frances, Mary, and Elizabeth.

The family would stay in Dr. Clark's house, but with father gone, how would they make rent? Paul was not entirely without means and resources, but the future seemed to hold little but a harsh inheritance.

CHAPTER 4

Foes

In which our hero launches into the troubled
waters of business, learns the many frustrations
of regulation and taxation, and then leaves it
all behind to fight the encroaching French.

Since hitting the Boston shore, Paul Revere's father forged his world from silver and gold. He bequeathed his son a fully functioning smithy, complete with tools, designs, molds, and customers. But Paul, who would one day become the most acclaimed goldsmith in America, was legally barred from taking up his father's tongs and hammers.

The law said that Paul had to finish his apprenticeship and strike more than a year off the calendar before he could become a legal shop owner. Had to be twenty-one for that. It was ten shillings' worth of skin off his nose every month the government caught him in breach.[1] He couldn't afford that, but neither could he afford to wait seventeen months to work. The family bills wouldn't keep, and the farmers who crossed Boston Neck every morning freighted with food for the locals were unimpressed by notes of credit.

Thank God for mom. The law exempted widows from the apprenticeship rules. Deborah probably stood up and stepped in as the official keeper of the store. Paul and younger brother Thomas could do the work, but mom would lend legal cover.

Paul might also have smoothed his legal bumps by taking in a temporary partner. Journeymen sometimes worked with Apollos. They had the training but no shops of their own. Paul's trouble might have been an opportunity for a craftsman in need of employment.

And then there was Nathaniel Hurd. The Reveres had a good relationship with the talented smith. Some speculate that he might have helped out temporarily. As far as polishing off his apprenticeship, Paul could do worse. Hurd was a gifted engraver, and later Paul would put the skill to famous and infamous use.[2]

However they coped, it was tough going. Money was so tight that Paul and the family had to stretch the rent with rum, fish, and silver work for the landlord. Making do was hard, and it was going to get harder.

Around this time, the Massachusetts General Court pushed an excise tax on the consumption of wine, rum, tea, and other goods. Boston merchants dodged previous sales taxes, so the new law put the onus of obedience on consumers themselves, requiring householders to swear an oath regarding how much their families had consumed of the taxable goods. Legislators could see that enforcement would be a pain, so the bill empowered officers to levy fines without trial.[3]

Word about the bill was contagious. Essayists and pamphleteers marshaled an army of words. Printing presses spit pages in a stream. Rumor, chatter, and gossip carried word from the pub, to the shop, to the docks, to the church. Mayhew preached a sermon titled "A Plea for the Poor and Distressed." Rev. Samuel Cooper of Brattle Street Church hit the same notes and italicized his concern by calling legislators "bastards" for the hardship their bill would inflict upon the poor.[4] The pseudonymous "Thomas Thumb, Esq." penned a satire that irked legislators so much they jailed the suspected printer and authorized the hangman to burn his pamphlet.[5] Still, the protests worked; the bill was defeated.[6]

Taxes play the villain in most any story of colonial America. Protests of the Excise Bill were a foretaste of things to come.

While the English settled up and down the eastern seaboard, rooting homes in the windswept bays and fertile inlets, the French came, too, settling farther north in Canada from where they descended into the Ohio River Valley. Originally the Adirondack and Appalachian Mountains prevented the settlers from butting into each other, but the English weren't about to stay on their side and hiked westward over the peaks, bringing these citizens of rival powers into uneasy and bumpy intersections. As one writer put it, "Even in times of peace the neighborhood of these nationalities on a long and ill-defined frontier was not always conducive to good fellowship, and in time of war furnished occasion for many acts of hostility and bloodshed."[7] The time of war was near.

In 1754 representatives from each government met to evict the other from the Ohio River Valley. It went badly—ambush, blood, and more—and both nations began fortifying strategic positions and outposts along their gauzy frontiers in what was soon to be known as the French and Indian War.[8]

The following year, the Brits implemented a bold plan. They gathered four regiments of regulars, provincial volunteers, and Indian allies, and waged offensives against French installments at Crown Point on Lake Champlain, the Forks of the Ohio River, Lake Ontario, and the Nova Scotia frontier. Bold—and a bust. British commander General Edward Braddock bought it at the Forks, and the assaults on Crown Point ended in failure. Still, the British took a typically British approach: if at first you don't succeed, enlist more men and have another go next year.

Paul was part of the second assault.

Down came the commission from William Shirley, the British government's royal governor of Massachusetts. "To Paul

Revere, Gentleman," it said. "I do by these Presents reposing especial Trust and Confidence in your Loyalty, Courage, and good conduct, constitute and appoint you . . . to be Second Lieutenant of the Train of Artillery, to be employed in the intended Expedition against Crown Point. . . ."[9]

What surged in his heart and stirred in his breast? Young men are easy for the danger and romance of war, the chance for heroics and noble sacrifice at the point when their lives are left craving for struggles more meaningful than making rent. And rent was no doubt in his mind. Paul turned twenty-one a few months before receiving his commission. He was finally free to run his own shop. And there was money to be made for the first time in years. British troops and the merchants who served them got money circulating again like a surge of blood in a languid limb. Paul was poised to finally make some decent cash. Instead he trudged off to war. Not that he was neglecting his family. His soldier's salary wasn't great, but at more than £5 it was enough to cover his bills back home and leave extra for his mom and siblings. Three months' pay would take care of Dr. Clark for the whole year.[10]

It was May 1756. Kitted with knapsacks, canteens, and muskets, Revere's company marched to Albany, New York.[11] From there the Hudson River snaked northward into the heart of French Canadian territory. If they traced the typical route, they followed the serpent. The men rowed upriver until they hit rough rapids at a place called Half-Moon. They disembarked with their gear and supplies and hoofed it to Stillwater, where calm currents welcomed watercraft. Hulls halved waves as far as Saratoga, where waters again became impassable. Out went the supplies. Men shored it and carried their stores to Upper Falls. Back in the boats, they sailed a bit farther to Fort Edward. Out again with the supplies, this time for good. Now they lumbered, dirt and grass all the way, more than a dozen miles, until they reached Fort William Henry, a walled encampment built south of Crown Point on Lake George.[12]

Paul and the others walked into a mess. Latrines, tents, slaughterhouses, kitchens were all jammed together. One observer said the "camp is nastier than anything I could conceive." Not surprisingly, several hundred of the more than two thousand men on site were sick.[13]

Crown Point was located farther north on Lake Champlain, which is connected to Lake George. Dense vegetation rimmed the lakes, making a land assault problematic. Boats were the thing, so the fort commander, Colonel Jonathan Bagley, set his men to shipwork and busted their tails. "I have almost worn the men out," he explained to his commander in midsummer, "poor dogs."[14]

It wasn't just the work. What wounds the labor and the locale didn't inflict, the French and the Indians wreaked. Small raiding parties harried the English troops. Bagley sent out skulking parties to find and fend them off. As a second lieutenant, Revere might have led or served one or more of these expeditions. They were mostly fruitless. "[W]e can't catch one of the sons of b—s," said Bagley.[15]

And they couldn't get the army up to Crown Point either. Soon it was fall, and the war stopped for winter.

Paul started the hard march home. Years later he wrote about his Fort William Henry exploits. It's a short report; nothing happened. But in some ways it was the seedbed from which everything would later sprout.[16]

Once home, Paul settled down quickly to domestic pursuits, and not just reestablishing the goldsmithing business. While casting mugs and hammering salvers, Paul also turned his attentions to more pleasurable occupations.

Sarah Orne was just a year his junior. There's no certainty when the two became an item, but they were both North Enders and probably attended the Cockerel together. He likely knew her for several years. When did she first catch his eye? It is easy to imagine he had intentions before marching off to war. Maybe the thought of young "Sary," as he affectionately called her, filled his breast with bravery at one moment and ache as he pined for home the next. The thought of her face would certainly lighten the grim and fruitless months spent at Lake George or hiking through the wilderness, wondering if around every tree there might be an Indian or Frenchman ready to snatch his scalp.

Although the start of their relationship is unknown, their wedding date is a matter of record. And so is the birth of their first daughter. Married on 17 August 1757, Sarah gave birth to little Deborah on 8 April 1758—eight months being just inside the margin of error.[17]

The family addition pointed to a bigger math problem. There were now three Deborahs under the same roof, all of whom looked to Paul for support. And there were more mouths to feed. The whole lot was still sardined inside Dr. Clark's Fish Street rental and only seemed to grow. Subtraction was the trick, but elder sister Deborah was not yet married and showed no imminent prospects. Thomas lived there and apprenticed under Paul. The only relief in sight was that young John would soon leave to apprentice as a tailor. That would provide some needed space in their cramped home, but Paul would still have to pay for his brother's board.

Paul's stint at Fort William Henry ended before it developed any of the thrills of a James Fenimore Cooper story. But the disastrous siege and violent capture of Fort William Henry depicted in *The Last of the Mohicans* commenced only two weeks before his wedding.

On 3 August, the French commander surrounded the "poor dogs" holed up inside. Three days later, the artillery started pummeling the fort, devastating the defenses. It was over by the ninth. With no help coming, the new fort commander, Lieutenant Colonel George Munro, could do nothing but surrender.

The following day, 10 August, Munro marched his battered men out of the fort with a small French escort to make sure the terms of surrender were kept. They were not. Several hundred of the French Indian allies broke ranks and butchered the column of defeated British. They aimed their assault on the rear of the line, where most of the contingent from the Massachusetts militia marched. The attack was merciless and bloody. More than a hundred were killed and scalped, and some five hundred were taken hostage.[18]

Paul read the worst of it in the papers or heard the stories repeated in shocked and sober tones. "Our friends and brethren, extirpated, butchered, scalped," reported the *Boston Gazette*; "our fields, lain waste; our territories, possessed by those that hate us."[19]

But later the papers had better news. The Brits rallied the following year and captured the Canadian city of Louisbourg from the French. Volunteers started pouring back into the lists, including five thousand Bay Colony boys.[20] Anticipation of victory spread faster than troops could march—and they could quickstep it. The army moved with such alacrity that the *Gazette* warned its readers, "[I]t will be very difficult for a weekly news writer to keep pace."[21] Paul and the rest of Boston were left hanging on their seats.

What's happening?

Are we winning?

With the momentum of a string of stunning victories behind them, the English pushed farther in and forced the surrender of Montreal in September 1759. "We have the most joyful news of the surrender of the city of Montreal," heralded the *Gazette*, "and therewith the surrender of Canada."[22]

The chore was done, and hostilities were effectively over. As if they could follow the newsprint like inky paths into the very events, anxious Bostonians could relive the stirring moments of final triumph. Though the war was not formally over for a few years to come as the Europeans ironed out a peace treaty, the Americans—Paul among them—got down to business.

CHAPTER 5

Friends

*In which our hero hones his business acumen
along with his art, experimenting with novel
metallurgic methods and embellishments,
while still making time for compotation and
conviviality at the Green Dragon—and joining
an extraordinary society of immense secrecy.*

Along with shop and tools, Paul inherited needy customers. Though his records only go back as far as 1761, he was bending his elbows from the start—repairing, polishing, refurbishing old pieces and creating striking new pieces as well.

Branching out from the simple and elegant Queen Anne style that most New England smiths used, Paul experimented with the more ornate rococo style. Smiths in New York and Philadelphia favored rococo's bold embellishments—raised engravings of flowers, leaves, shells, even animal shapes. But Boston smiths, perhaps influenced by some vestigial Puritan austerity, weren't having it. Paul was, and he proved very skilled at it.

Rococo requires a lot of casting, molding, and engraving. Silver's ductility and malleability make that easy. Maybe too easy. Lacking an eye for beauty and the talent to execute, smiths could end up creating an expensive mess. Some rococo work is stylized and decorated to the point of caricature. Not Revere's. From all points in his career, Paul showed a sensibility that never stepped over the line into the gaudy.

One of the earliest pieces that displays his talents in the style is a salver crafted in 1760 for William White as a wedding gift to his first cousin, the merchant William Phillips. Phillips's grandfather had been a silversmith in Salem, and it is likely that his tastes reflected the fact. Paul rimmed the piece in leaves and seashells, rococo design elements placed and spaced with the Queen Anne's conservative aesthetic.[1] Another piece, a salver for Lucretia Chandler made the following year, shows a similar design, with deep-fluted scallops arranged around the rim and a finely engraved coat of arms in the center. Other items designed for Chandler are more adventurous (a pear-shaped cream pot and sugar bowl dense with floral scrollwork and budding vines),[2] but regardless of the customer or the piece—tall pot for serving coffee or squat cann for swilling beer—each item sports the same aesthetic: graceful loops and curves, precise chasing and engraving, balance in form and function.

Paul's real talent was the balancing act. Keeping up with silver fashion as successfully as he did while also refraining from being swept away by it highlights not only his skill as a craftsman, but also his handle on the market for his craft. This sort of business savvy would take him beyond mere artisan into the realm of entrepreneur.

Paul kept the family afloat and kept adding to it. Elder sister Deborah finally married and moved out in February 1759, in time to make room for another little Revere born to Sarah in 1760, this one named after Dad. The littlest Paul Revere, Paul Jr., arrived on the sixth of January and was baptized a week later at the Cockerel.[3]

Biographer Esther Forbes suggests that Paul might have been aloof in family life.[4] He certainly seems to have spent a lot of time socializing. Magnetism characterized Paul Revere's personality perhaps more than anything. There's every indication that he loved his wife and home, but he also frequented inns and taverns, joined clubs, and befriended many people high and low.

After a trying day at the trade, Paul often repaired to bastions of beer and brotherhood. Boston had so many taverns in operation (more than thirty) that one governor jested that every other house was an alehouse.[5] Besides church, the town knew no more important social center than the taproom of the local inn. At the ordinary, as a tavern or public house was then called, a person could find conversation, conviviality, and cups of Madeira, rum, beer, and flip (a popular cocktail made largely from beer, sweetened usually with sugar or molasses, fortified with a bit of rum, and then heated with a red-hot iron poker that was thrust into the mug, giving the mixture a highly desirable scorched and bitter taste). Several taverns occupied space in the North End. Some, like Salutation Tavern and the Green Dragon, were regular haunts for Revere. The former, on Salutation Alley by North Battery, and the latter, on Union Street, a stone's throw from Mill Pond, were about equal distance from his house. The ambience in each was much the same.

In he went.

Over the threshold, the sights and smells might trigger a sigh of relaxation or a smile of anticipation. The air was dense with the earthy aroma of tobacco, smoked in long and slender clay pipes by sailors and artisans. Smoke hung along the ceiling joists and mingled with thin, gray plumes from dim oil lamps that lit the space. The glowing hearth crackled, perhaps with a kettle of stew or a spit of pork. Maybe Paul showed up for a prearranged meeting, or maybe he lucked into a serendipitous moment with someone he hadn't seen in a few days or weeks—a customer like Nathaniel Fosdick, who remembered he needed such and such an item made or repaired. He might see his cousin Nathaniel Hitchborn or another friend, like Josiah Flagg, now a jeweler on Fish Street, maybe a local pastor or two, even Mayhew. Having retrieved a measure of rum or beer from Dame Catherine Kerr, proprietor of the Dragon, he would wander to a chair and get in a game of backgammon or linger among his friends and neighbors, listening, talking, exchanging ideas, reading the paper. Politics, religion, family news, town gossip—it was all fair game to the tipplers and taverngoers.

Because they provided space to meet, usually private rooms adjoining or in the floor above taprooms, political and social clubs often met in taverns—including one Paul was very soon to join, the Masons.

Originally founded as a medieval trade union of stonemasons, as the Renaissance gave way to the Enlightenment, the secretive body transmogrified into something of a gentleman's club.

Paul's first exposure to the group probably came in the military. One of his commanders, Richard Gridley, was a Mason and received permission to start a military lodge at Lake George. Back home, Paul joined in September 1760 and by the end of January 1761 had advanced through the three degrees of membership: entered apprentice, then fellow craft, finally master Mason. He was the first to officially join St. Andrew's, a newly established lodge, as its chartering paperwork had only just arrived.

"These men, heirs of the scientific revolution, were interested in science, philosophy and history," writes scholar Edith J. Steblecki. "By imbuing the ancient rituals and traditions of the mason's craft with a higher moral tone, these men formulated an organization that provided a sense of social order, encouraged stable values, offered a hierarchy of merit within which members could attain status through instruction. . . ."[6]

In Paul's day (though not so in later times), the Masons pursued these aims within the fold of Christian orthodoxy. Masonic oaths then used language like "You shall be a True Man to God, and to the Holy Church; and that you use no Error, nor Heresy by your Understanding, or by the teaching of Men." And "You must serve God according to the best of your Knowledge and Institution, and be a true Liege Man to the King, and help and assist any Brother as far as your Ability will allow. By the Contents of the Sacred Writ you will perform this oath." The Masonic creed held that men were naturally equal and achieved rank not through class or inheritance, but through learning and merit—a worldview that resonated within Puritan New England with its strong ethic of striving and work.[7]

The decision made back in the Old World to solder the Revere fortunes to goldsmithing had a substantial impact on Paul's life in the New. Goldsmiths were the princes of artisans. Virtually alone among mechanics, as artisans often called themselves, they worked with precious metals. That meant they had to be trustworthy people and trusted by the people who mattered the most in their communities—people like the Hutchinsons, people with enough wealth to require their services more than occasionally. In that rare position, they tended to straddle traditional classes, bridging the working class and the leisure class. This fact was amplified by something afoot in the culture.

The New World invited novelty and experimentation, not only for, say, repressed religious sects, but also for new class structures. A hint of this is in Paul's 1756 commission in the Massachusetts militia, addressed to "Paul Revere, Gentleman." It's a throwaway compliment today, but in Revere's day *gentleman* was a description of social status, reserved mainly for men

Paul's good friend James Warren.
Library of Congress.

of land, wealth, or title. Revere was none of those things, but in the New World the social ladder was as short as it was unstable. Class barriers were real, but not insurmountable. By excelling in one's craft and rising in the esteem of his neighbors, a man had a shot at going from the lower sort to the middle sort, and maybe even to the upper sort. Revere would butt his head on that social ladder from time to time, but the fact that he always felt the ability to keep moving upward in his life is telling.

Because of the high-minded Masonic ideals of merit and inherent human worth, within the bounds of Masonic relationships, class counted for less than it did on the outside. That meant that Paul's circle was expanding beyond his middle-class and artisan confines. More than anything, his membership in the Masons connected him to the men who would soon lead the resistance to overreaches of Crown and Parliament, men like Samuel Adams, James Otis, John Hancock, and Joseph Warren.

In 1761, St. Andrew's lodge met twenty-six times. Paul missed only one meeting.[8] In one of the other twenty-five meetings he met Joseph Warren, a man with whom he developed a great friendship. Warren had just finished a teaching gig in Roxbury, the neighboring town, and come to Boston to apprentice in medicine. He signed on with Dr. James Lloyd, a pioneer of sorts, and learned to diagnose illnesses, suture (instead of sear) wounds, mix and administer medicines, inoculate against smallpox (a controversial treatment at the time), and amputate limbs with more care than the average practitioner of the hack-and-saw business.[9] But life wasn't all anatomy studies, house calls, and the like. The Masons opened up a social circle for Warren that included not only Revere, but Paul's cousin Nathaniel Hitchborn and in wider orbits men like Adams and Otis.[10]

The Masons also helped Paul in his business endeavors. His life was very much about bridges. He was a social bug, and the Masons expanded his social and professional sphere. He seemed to easily ingratiate himself to people of all walks. Business started to gleam. He now made items for fellow Masons, including Masonic medals, or jewels, as they are called. In January 1761 he made a Masonic medal for James Graham. The following year he made medals for Richard Pulling.

Not everything was charity and brotherly love, of course.

He was a hatter named Thomas Fosdick and in May 1761 brought charges against Revere for "assaulting and beating the complainant [according to] the warrant on file."[11] It was a family affair. Fosdick was married to Paul's cousin, Frances Hitchborn. They'd tied the knot while Paul was busy defending the realm against the French. Fosdick apparently did little to ingratiate himself to the family during the campaign. Paul "was not by nature a tavern brawler," writes Esther Forbes, venturing that he "[p]robably . . . had good reason for his antipathy."[12]

So there was Paul, standing before the black-robed and bewigged Judge Richard Dana, justice of the peace, explaining his part in breaking it.

Paul answered not guilty when prompted to plea. Dana listened to testimony, reviewed the facts, and decided otherwise. "Defendant pleads not guilty," wrote Dana, but "after a full hearing it appears that he is guilty." Dana had seen a lot worse in his days, however, and didn't seem overly perturbed with Paul's actions. After assessing a small fine and court costs, he ordered him to "keep the peace and be of good behavior" and asked two of his fellows to post bond to make sure he stayed in line. One was Paul's friend Joshua Brackett, a coppersmith. The other was one of Paul's customers and Tom's own brother, Nathaniel Fosdick.[13]

Given the light fine and Nathaniel's siding with Paul, it's a safe bet that Tom had it coming. That's even more likely considering the rarity of Paul throwing punches.

Fistfights are not typically associated with social climbers, which Paul surely was.

Paul was a man of some standing, something he wouldn't be if he were living in Britain, and that standing would only increase as the opportunities multiplied for him to excel in his dealings and display courage and resourcefulness. With his business picking up and the political struggles taking shape in Boston, those opportunities were on the rise.

CHAPTER 6

Grudges

*In which the narrative swerves afield to discover
the key role that smuggling played in the discord
between England and America, with special focus
on the so-called and much-loathed writs
of assistance and how Thomas Hutchinson
came to make enemies of all the wrong men.*

Thomas Hutchinson didn't mean to irk his neighbors. He just did. Hutchinson's alliances with the upper crust and ruling establishment tied him to the downfall of the land bank and the financial and political ruination of Samuel Adams's father. Battling debt collectors for years afterward, Adams never forgave Hutchinson. And now in the Otis family, Hutchinson had another bad father-son combo that was sure to cause him trouble.

But first, some backstory.

Trade linked Britain to its colonies, and the Acts of Trade and Navigation (Navigation Acts for short) governed the linkage. Strengthening British commerce against foreign powers was the goal. Britain's mercantilist system aggrandized as much production, trade, and profit for itself as possible. Colonies were instruments in the enterprise, providing goods for British markets and markets for British goods.[1]

The trick was keeping other nations out of the picture. "If we allow France and Holland to supply them with fabric," one Englishman explained England's attitude—and just about any other importable good could be substituted here, tea, molasses, or wine—"we may just as well give up all ideas of having colonies at all."[2] The Navigation Acts mandated virtually all trade be funneled through Britain or British outposts to tax and regulate goings-on in keeping with British interests. But as philosopher and economist Adam Smith later observed, "Not many people are scrupulous about smuggling, when, without perjury, they can find any easy and safe opportunity for doing so."[3]

Firebrand Sam Adams.
Library of Congress.

It's an old story. From day one, the English themselves flouted English trade laws. After King Edward III levied a tax on wool in the thirteenth century, ports in Sussex and Kent started smuggling the stuff and other restricted goods as well.[4] England's endless bays, inlets, and coves provided plenty of places to "run" goods to shore away from the reach of customs agents. Loading contraband by lantern and moonlight, British smugglers were called *owlers*, and their wee-hours business was so lucrative that seaside farmers had trouble competing for labor. While planters struggled finding enough hands to harvest crops from their fields, hands aplenty harvested cases of tobacco, rum, wine, and tea from the holds of sloops and schooners.[5]

The Crown cracked down. In the 1660s, Charles II authorized search warrants called *writs of assistance* that allowed officers of the Crown a wide berth to nose around shipyards, warehouses, and homes for contraband. "Assistance" meant that customs men could enlist the help of the sheriff in nabbing the ne'er-do-wells.[6]

Increased enforcement meant increased resistance. Customs men were so loathed that during one period in England, before the American Revolution, more than two hundred and fifty were assaulted. Some were horsewhipped; half a dozen were murdered. Excise houses were torched, and full-blown riots broke out. Tax historian Charles Adams even tells of a collector who was dragged from his bed and slain right in front of his helpless family.[7]

Britain's biggest problem was with the Dutch.[8] Smuggling with Holland was so pervasive that the English even imported the word *smokkelen* from their rival.[9] Holland had freewheeling trade laws and generally low taxes, and that meant that British merchants could get a better deal importing Dutch goods. Take tea. By the 1760s, America annually washed more than a million pounds down its collective gullet, so Britain, which produced the stuff in India, should have been swimming in revenues from the trade. But no. Parliament's taxes doubled the cost of the British East India Company's tea compared to that of its Dutch rivals. Conservative estimates suggest that more than three-quarters of American tea was smuggled, and most of the smuggled stuff came from Holland. One of Massachusetts' governors wrote back to Britain that "there is a great quantity of Dutch Teas stirring about [Boston]," adding a colorful detail: "carts and other carriages are heard to be continually going about in the dead of night, which can be for no other purpose than smuggling."[10] The practice was so widespread that when the famed evangelist George Whitefield visited the colonies in 1740, he preached against it. "What will become of you," he said, "who cheat the King of his taxes?"[11]

But Whitefield was pushing a tough message up a steep hill. The colony had a long, entrenched history of ignoring Britain's trade laws. More than sixty years before Whitefield's visit, a British official named Edward Randolph sent a lengthy report to London from Massachusetts. Here's an excerpt:

There is no notice taken of the act of navigation, plantation, or any other lawes made in England for the regulation of trade. All nations having free liberty to come into their ports and vend their commodities, without any restraint; and in this as well as in other things, that government would make the world believe they are a free state and doe act in all matters accordingly.[12]

That was back in 1676, but even as rules tightened and adherence increased in succeeding decades, smuggling proved easy and the incentives great. "Official" practice even allowed for it, and authorities only partially enforced the Navigation Acts. Customs men and merchants came to a more or less comfortable (if illegal) truce that involved reporting some goods and smuggling the rest.[13]

But by 1760, the Crown made a renewed effort to curb smugglers. Newly appointed Governor Francis Bernard was happy to help—if mainly for personal reasons.

Bernard, a jowly man with a long, straight nose, was fifty years of age—and badly in debt—when he took the helm in Massachusetts in August 1760. He was in the hole from the beginning when he took the governorship of New Jersey after moving his large family to America. It wasn't ostentatious, but his lifestyle contained a bit more life and style than he could realistically afford, and he took the Massachusetts job only because he was desperate. He continued to struggle and had financial trouble moving his wife and children, including several unemployed sons, to his new post in Massachusetts. All of that would change, he hoped. The pay was meager (only £1,200 sterling a year, and it cost him a third of that just to buy his commission), but there were other benefits.[14] For one, Boston was an urbane setting for the "refined conversation and amusements that arise from letters, arts, and sciences" that he craved.[15]

Knowingly or not, the Bay Colony played to Bernard's soft spot. Meeting him on the road into Boston with a parade of cavalry, coaches loaded with the town's best-wigged set, and members of the Governor's Council (the upper house of the legislature), Bernard was escorted to the courthouse, thronged by cheering subjects and saluting militia.[16] Who could refuse the adoration?

But there was another windfall for Bernard. Orders came from both the secretary of state and the king himself to clamp down on smuggling.[17] To encourage enforcement, the law provided the governor a third of whatever goods or money was seized. For the financially strapped Bernard, it was all the encouragement he needed. "He was determined to get every penny to which his office entitled him," according to historian Bernard Bailyn.[18]

But it wasn't going to be easy. A month after his arrival, Governor Bernard walked into a controversy. The Superior Court's chief justice, Stephen Sewall, died, and it was up to Bernard to appoint his replacement.

The post had already been promised to James Otis's father by the two preceding governors. Otis, who was then the advocate general, met with Hutchinson about his father's appointment; the two knew each other, and Otis thought that by lobbying his colleague, he could then perhaps remind the governor of the long-standing promise. The two men sat down together, spindly Hutchinson with his narrow face and undersized chin, and thickset Otis with his bulging cheeks and stocky neck. In the meeting Hutchinson praised the

The excitable James Otis, lifelong foe of Thomas Hutchinson. *US History Images.*

elder Otis's qualifications and downplayed any personal interest in the job. When Otis left, he had every reason to believe that his father would receive the post.

But Bernard wasn't having any. He rejected the elder Otis, determined to have someone he knew could be relied upon to back the Crown in any case that might come up. For him, that meant Hutchinson—despite Hutchinson's disinterest in the post and lack of qualifications. Bernard insisted, and Otis be hanged, Hutchinson took the new appointment in November 1760.[19]

When word got back to Otis, he snapped. He certainly waivered from time to time, but from that moment on, he opposed Bernard and Hutchinson at most every opportunity. And one was quick to arise.

The Massachusetts Superior Court issued writs of assistance to applicants. The writs authorized customs men to break into ships, shops, cellars, warehouses, vaults, and even homes and poke around for "uncustomed" goods, wares, or merchandise—anything on which duties had not been paid or otherwise properly handled.[20] Unlike typical warrants, these weren't issued to search a particular place for a particular thing, usually for a limited time. These warrants were open-ended and applied to anyplace the official's nose might lead. They were particularly irksome to merchants and ship captains whose activities (both legal and not) were frequently disrupted—if not actually thwarted—by customs officers.

While the court issued the writs, their authority extended from the king. When the king died, so did the authority of writs and commissions given in his reign. Like fruit withering on a dead vine, they were valid for only six months after his passing. Start counting. King George II died in October 1760. News reached Boston in December.

Here was Otis's chance. Customs would have to apply for new writs. Sixty-plus merchants petitioned for a hearing to argue against the writs, among them Nathaniel Wheelwright, William Molineaux, and Daniel Malcolm. Otis resigned his government post and instead represented the petitioners. One customs official, Thomas Lechmere, the surveyor general of the customs office, counterpetitioned, and the fight was on.[21]

The council room in the State House was crammed on 24 February 1761. Everyone was there for the showdown, including Sam Adams's younger cousin, John, who kept notes of the proceedings. Local lawyers as well as out-of-towners crowded the space, intently listening to each word. Otis and Oxenbridge Thatcher argued against the writs, Attorney General Jeremiah Gridley for them. It was bone-chilling outside, and the five judges, Hutchinson among them, decked in their scarlet robes, broad bands, and massive wigs, sat closest to the fire.[22] Otis's fevered oration warmed the room on its own.

He was forthright. "This writ is against the fundamental principles of law," he claimed. "A man . . . is as secure in his house as a prince in his castle."[23] He was forceful, declaring that "an act [of Parliament] against the constitution is void; an act against natural equity is void. . . ."[24] He was also flip. Parliament had banned iron manufacturing in the colonies; Otis sneered, what is the "noble lord's proposal, that we should send our horses to England to be shod?"[25] The audacity was electrifying. He was actually challenging the authority of Parliament. John Adams was so captivated that his note taking suffered.

The judges knew from where Otis pulled his argument. Drawing on the legal theories of Lord Edward Coke, Otis challenged the legality of the writ, then—importantly—moved to attack the Navigation Acts themselves. If the Navigation Acts violated the English Constitution, then they were bumfodder.[26] Coke, England's most celebrated jurist, might have been shocked to see his positions used in such a flagrant attack on British sovereignty, but Otis's use was only advancing the argument, doing what Coke himself had called growing new corn from old fields.[27] Given the outcome, maybe the better metaphor lies in Jesus' proverb, his warning about putting new wine in old wineskins. The result in the case of Otis and the writs was predictable— the skins burst. Not yet, but soon.

Despite Otis's eloquence, his rhetorical assault, and his carefully constructed case, Hutchinson wasn't buying. Forget all the constitutional questions and the ultimate legality, for Hutchinson the entire thing came down to a technicality that required some fact-finding into how the matter was handled back in England. Until this was discovered, the ruling was shelved and the parties left to stew. He might have narrowly saved the day. As he later wrote, "the court seemed inclined to refuse to grant [the writs]; but I prevailed with my brethren to continue the cause until the next term. . . ."[28]

The delay worked, and the facts proved as Hutchinson hoped. In November 1761, the court reconvened and, after rehearing the arguments, ruled and validated the writs.

It was just one more stroke of ignominy as far as Otis was concerned. Hutchinson was too aloof to see it, but he was trending in a bad way. The editorial focus of the *Boston Gazette* took an important turn. The paper was filled no more with stories of the bellicose French; the ink started to fly at Hutchinson and his circle.

The court closed session in November, and in December Lechmere and his customs officers got their writs. At the same time Paul's lodge mates elected him to his first Masonic office, junior deacon. Paul had been traveling in Masonic circles for more than a year at this point. He'd heard enough and seen enough to know: Hutchinson was picking the wrong enemies.

CHAPTER 7

Pox

*The year 1762 begins well for our hero, but the
smallpox returns and runs rampant through
Boston, a ravage shortly followed by a novel
tax measure that for the first time set the
colonies against the imperial government.*

The year 1762 was very good for Paul Revere. It
started with the birth of his second daughter, Sarah,
named after her mother, on 3 January. She was baptized, if
records mean anything, immediately thereafter.[1]

Professionally things were looking up as well. Revere's
shop hours were filled with polishing plates, refurbishing
tankards, and doing other maintenance and repair work.
He also churned out a steady stream of little items such as
spoons, rings, thimbles, buttons, and buckles that cinched
everything from britches to girdles to shoes.[2] Most of the

work was done in silver, but some of the daintier items were done in gold. Paul could work with just about anything. In February 1762, Revere fixed silver handles to "two shells for spoons." And later that year he fashioned a branding iron for his cousin William Hitchborn. Never locked into a particular program or way of doing business, Revere was always flexible and willing to try something new if it meant amusement, a challenge, or a paycheck. An example of all three: one customer requested, and Paul created, a silver chain for his pet squirrel.[3]

Revere's flexibility allowed him to take on work that other goldsmiths might miss. In 1762 (or thereabouts) he ventured into copperplate engraving. The image he created, the aforementioned depiction of the North Battery, was crafted to illustrate a military certificate. Revere's copperplate engraving never rose to the heights of fine art, but it did pay the bills from time to time.

What did soar was his reputation for the high-relief rococo engraving, called *repoussé*, that he worked for such items as teapots and sugar bowls. He proved so talented in its execution that his work was sought by other smiths. They were reliant on his skills to fulfill work for their own clients. Old family friend Nathaniel Hurd outsourced work to him in 1762. So did another silversmith, Benjamin Green. Paul's ledgers are full of such dealings. One smith, Samuel Minott, must have been especially fond of his ornamental engraving and chasing because he came to Paul on several occasions for orders. In some cases Paul would even make items for resale in other smiths' shops.[4]

So 1762 was a year for advancement, but 1763 was a different story. The war boom went bust, and Boston slowly reverted to economic bedlam, no small part of it exacerbated by England's trade laws. Credit got tight as trade slowed and in some cases stopped. Paul's income that year dropped almost £200, from £294 to £95.[5] And the problems were not all his own. In December 1763 things went from bad to disastrously worse. The pox had returned.[6]

Smallpox was a death stalker in colonial Boston, killing hundreds, even thousands, at a time. Fevers burned and boiled, disfiguring pustules burst, and oozing skin stuck to sheets and blankets and bandages. The disease prowled through the streets and among the shops, reaching into the homes of both rich and poor. Europeans had lived with the pox for centuries and had generally developed resistance by its constant attack. But as generations expanded in the New World in relative isolation, smallpox could—as it did in Boston in the 1720s—scythe away great swaths of the community.

Knowing the disease spread person to person through some sort of contagion, Boston government mandated quarantine at the first hint of the pox. Affected boats were locked down at the docks, and the sick were confined indoors, with flags and guards posted outside. But with an incubation period of almost two weeks, a victim could infect scores before authorities could lock him away.

Unwilling to take any chances with the disease, Boston's leading merchant, Thomas Hancock, and nephew John, split town, elaborate wardrobes and precious possessions in tow. They set up shop at Harvard College to ride things out. The General Court did the same.[7] Not that they were entirely out of harm's way. A fire jumped the hearth in the college library and reduced the structure to cinders and ash. Governor Bernard and members of the legislature fought the blaze, but Thomas Hancock's valuables burned along with thousands of books and the building itself.[8]

Revere's situation looked better. At least at first. The day after New Year's Day, 1764, Paul took a big order from Joseph Barnard for a silver cup and tankard—a single job worth more than twenty pounds.[9] Two days into the new year and he'd already logged a sale worth a fifth his takings the previous year.

But that same day, a sailor recently in from Newfoundland, the man who brought the pox to town, died. He was staying right there on Fish Street in Paul's neighborhood. The selectmen ordered all the proper doings: remains laid in a tarred sheet and coffin; corpse conveyed to its burial after midnight; apartments scrubbed; bedding taken away by boat. Clothes, possessions, dwelling, anything he had touched was smoked with brimstone and frankincense, and his house was aired out from midnight to dawn for two consecutive nights.[10]

It wasn't enough.

On the night of the sailor's burial, a woman said she caught "the smell of the Small Pox." Soon she had the disease, and others did as well. First three families. Then five. Then twenty. Most all near Paul's house on Fish Street.[11]

By the end of the month, the town selectmen were meeting about the outbreak every day, even on Sundays in the evening after church.[12]

Then one of Paul's children showed symptoms. Revere appeared before the town selectmen 6 February. The authorities wanted him to confine the child to a hospital away from the town center and, more important for Paul, away from the family. Nothing doing, he said. Sarah was nearly eight months pregnant, and there was no way he was going to consign one of his "little lambs" to die in a hospital away from her care. The feistiness that ended in Tom Fosdick's bruises was now marshaled to defend his family's interests. Unable to budge him, the selectmen quarantined the entire family at home behind a red flag—all except Paul, who, showing no signs of infection, was not allowed to enter the house.[13]

It wasn't long before Paul's Hitchborn cousins got it. So did the family of his friend Josiah Flagg.[14] By month's end, enough people had either passed out of danger or passed out of this world that only seven families were then afflicted—all were North Enders.[15] But the abatement was only a lull. In a matter of weeks, the disease flared like the Harvard fire, and a third of the residents fled the city.[16] The dead stacked up so fast that the selectmen now ordered the church sextons and gravediggers to round up the corpses and bury them "without the usual Solemnities of a Funeral. . . ."[17] The town's doctors, including Joseph Warren and Benjamin Church, had their hands full, treating the sick and inoculating the well.[18]

By the end of March the Reveres were out of danger. The disease had run its course in the family, though it continued to ravage the town through the spring. Paul didn't seem to get it at all.

He hadn't taken an order in several weeks, but there was still cause to celebrate. Sarah was delivered, and little Mary had joined the family on the final day of the month and was baptized the first day of the next.[19] Orders started coming in again, and the family finances improved. But things were happening outside Clark's Wharf that would complicate things for Paul.

As Boston was dealing with the pox, the boys of the St. Andrew's Masonic Lodge were making a deal of their own. In January they voted to buy a permanent meeting house. They chose the Green Dragon, and the negotiations took place while the Revere family was in quarantine.[20] Eight Masons pulled together to buy the tavern, and one of the group petitioned the selectmen for permission to operate the tavern. He got it. Distracted with the pox, Paul was not part of this committee, but he did join the stewards charged with the tavern's upkeep and governance in May.[21]

He took the position of junior warden, several ranks ahead of junior deacon. The job required collecting dues at meetings, vetting visitors, and introducing new candidates. The group met upstairs in the Long Room. No doubts as to what filled the conversation.

Wars are a lot of things, none of them cheap. In the eight years between 1755 and when the peace treaty with France was finally inked in 1763, Britain's debt ballooned by £50 million—from £72 million to £122 million. Interest alone was £5 million a year. Parliament also needed to maintain an army in their newly won territory to keep the French from getting any ideas. Ten thousand troops would cost roughly £220,000 a year. Asking Brits at home to pay for the army stationed in America, on top of all they were already paying (which was a lot), seemed out of the question, so Parliament started looking for change in the cushions, and they started poking around in the colonies.

Smugglers reigned, and despite the writs of assistance, incentives to seize, and urgings of the Crown, the customs men weren't gaining enough ground. Across all the colonies collectors brought in £1,800, and their salaries cost £7,500—hardly earning their keep. Parliament directed the navy to begin intercepting smugglers.

But even if smuggling ceased, there wouldn't be enough revenue. The Navigation Acts were primarily to regulate trade—directing it, governing it, lubing the lucre and helping it slide swiftly toward merchants in Merry Old England. Now the government needed to pass acts that raised revenue as their primary function. One such act was the 1764 Sugar Act. The 1733 Molasses Act was designed to keep colonial distillers from using French molasses. The exorbitant taxes acted as a fence to direct molasses purchases into English channels. But now the Brits were more concerned with funds than keeping the colonists from doing business with the French. So the 1764 Sugar Act dropped the import duty on molasses—lower taxes are more likely to be paid. It's counterintuitive, but that was a problem. As the colonists saw it, for the first time Parliament, in which they had no representation, was trying to tax them. A mere duty or fee for the purposes of regulation they could tolerate. But this was different.

The radical elements of Boston politics now start coming into sharp relief.

In May 1764, Samuel Adams was commissioned to write the town meeting's instructions to the Massachusetts legislature. He focused on the Sugar Act. If the new law passed, he said, "it will be scarce possible for us to earn our Bread." But there was even more curdle in the cream; new taxes, he said, would serve as pretext for still further taxation: "For if our Trade may be taxed why not our Lands? Why not the Produce of our Lands & every thing we possess or make use of?" And those taxes would essentially be illegal: "This . . . annihilates our Charter Right to govern & tax ourselves—It strikes at our Brittish Privileges. . . . If Taxes are laid upon us in any shape without our having legal Representation where they are laid, are we not reduced from the Character of free Subjects to the miserable State of a tributary of Slaves?"[22]

Otis jumped in with a pamphlet called *The Rights of the British Colonies Asserted and Proved*, saying much the same:

I can see no reason to doubt, but that the imposition of taxes, whether on trade, or land, or houses, or ships, on real or personal, fixed or floating property, in the colonies, is absolutely irreconcileable with the rights of the Colonists, as British subjects, and as men. I say men, for in a state of nature, no man can take my property from me, without my consent: If he does, he deprives me of my liberty, and makes me a slave.[23]

British authorities didn't look at it this way, of course. Agents for the colonists protested, but Parliament never entertained the objections. The Americans and their spokesmen may have had tongues of silver and lips of gold, but in London it seemed as if all the ears were made of wood. No one heard a word of it.

CHAPTER 8

Riots

*In which our hero struggles through
the vagaries and vicissitudes of trade,
while the Stamp Act is foisted upon
the unsuspecting populace of the American
colonies, prompting Bostonians to act
in a manner both violent and shocking,
giving birth, as it were, to the Sons of Liberty.*

The Sugar Act became law in September 1764—new costs at a time when revenues were low. Military contracts from the recent war had dried up, and troops had taken their blow money back to Britain and other parts of the empire as they left Boston. Back in 1733 Apollos's finances suffered in the wake of the Molasses Act. The same was now true for Paul. It was autumn, and Boston's economy fell like bronzed and coppered leaves. Merchants held orders, creditors called debts, bankruptcies spread.[1]

Ever the entrepreneur, Paul and longtime friend Josiah Flagg took a gamble on a publishing project. Flagg had a knack for music and pulled together a rare collection of hymns, most of which had never before graced American ears. Paul engraved the copper plates and printed the pages. In the preface Flagg and Revere admit indebtedness "to the other Side of the Atlantick chiefly, for our Tunes" but then inject a little homespun pride that "the Paper on which they are printed is the Manufacture of our own Country."[2] They advertised the book in the Boston papers in November.[3] *Dear God, let it sell!*

The gamble was mainly Paul's. He charged Flagg £150 for his half of the engraving and printing expenses, but Flagg already owed him more than £50 at the time.[4] The situation didn't look promising.

But then came a stroke of good luck. In December Paul took a big job. Captain Joseph Goodwin ordered, among other things, a teapot and sugar dish. The gig paid £15. Thanks to the order, Paul ended the troubled year at £102, up from £95 in 1763.[5]

Come the new year, Paul still had hymnbooks to sell. He and Josiah advertised again in January and February 1765.[6] Not an uncommon problem in publishing—they misjudged. Sure, Bostonians could have used a few pleasant strains. But who had the money?

The question buzzed up and down the streets and alleys. People started asking in earnest after January when Boston merchant, war speculator, and banker Nathaniel Wheelwright defaulted and left creditors and depositors holding almost £180,000 in worthless IOUs. Few took the news well. One merchant stroked and died in his lawyer's office. Others went bankrupt—almost sixty before autumn, another seventy-five over the next few years. The *Boston Gazette* compared Wheelwright to a crashing comet whose "fiery Tail . . . swept lesser Stars Down from their sev'ral Orbits." Boston newspapers began to tally and report the new bankruptcies along with other common vital stats, like the weekly number of baptisms and burials. "This was like an earthquake," Governor Bernard wrote London.[7]

Damage spread beyond the bankrupted money boys. With merchants on ice, artisans lost many of their customers and closed up shop. Debts went unpaid as shop doors slammed and jail locks clanged. Shipping dwindled too. Horrible storms racked the bay in March, damaging wharves and crippling ships.[8] What damage the general economy and Mother Nature couldn't inflict, the law took care of. With the navy now intercepting smugglers, strict prosecution walloped trade. By year's end the number of ships leaving from Boston to Europe or the West Indies dropped by 80 percent. Those jobs that survived paid half the previous rate.[9] (To avoid his troubles, Wheelwright boarded one of the few ships heading to the West Indies; he died in disgrace a year later on the island of Guadeloupe.)

Paul got work, but it was minimal, and he utilized sideline skills for it. In March, the Massachusetts legislature commissioned him to "cut the view of a hemp mill Model" (that is, engrave a printing plate), which had been invented by Josiah's father, Gershom Flagg. Josiah couldn't pay Paul what he owed him, but the relationship seems to have helped Paul score the job. He engraved the plate and printed four hundred copies. These were included in Edmund Quincy's pamphlet *Treatise of Hemp Husbandry*. Paul picked up forty-four shillings for the job.[10] Not much, but it was better than nothing. Only just. By April Paul rented out part of his shop to pick up an additional £4 for the year.[11] Despite all this, the real shock that month was the death of Paul's littlest daughter, Mary.[12] She'd been born just thirteen months before, at the end of the small-pox outbreak. Perhaps her health was never very robust. However predictable or inevitable, the burden on the family must have been unbearable.

Parliament had another scheme to raise funds in America. Earlier, it had floated the idea of the Stamp Act along with introduction of the Sugar Act, but let it cool. Then they cranked up the heat in the spring of 1765. The idea was to charge a fee on almost any transaction in which paper was exchanged. That meant legal papers, newspapers, even playing cards. Everything had to bear an official stamp, which official stamp men would sell. The fees would jump the sea to Parliament's purse.

Parliament passed the Stamp Act in March 1765, but the colonists didn't find out for a couple of months. By the time they did know, the economic problems of the Sugar Act were being felt everywhere. Unemployment, reduced trade, bankruptcies. Nursing their wounds, people looked for someone to blame. The rumor mill churned, and Thomas Hutchinson went in headfirst. Out came the hamburgered remains of his reputation.

Hutchinson opposed the Stamp Act, but detractors didn't believe him. They said that his opposition was lukewarm, that it was calculated to appear as if he were opposed while all the time he was actually cheering its passage. Opponents continued to dredge up old sins—his opposition to paper money and the land bank, support of the writs of assistance, his thick portfolio of public offices (he did in fact hold several offices at the same time). Otis and Adams, both wounded by Hutchinson in the past, were the prime dredgers. Paul would have heard the same scuttlebutt in his circle. Hutchinson had this going against him as well: his brother-in-law, Andrew Oliver, picked up the appointment to Bay Colony stamp master and soon threw up a brick building at his South End dock. The assumption was that it was Oliver's Stamp Office.

Some, like the fire brigade, were prepared to take it sitting down—literally. They agreed to let the heap burn if it caught fire. Others were more active in their protest. A few of Paul's friends and customers decided to offer organized resistance. John Avery, one of his customers, and Thomas Crafts, a lodge brother, joined with several others in a group called the Loyal Nine. Henry Welles, thought to be a member of the Nine, was a lodge brother as well. *Boston Gazette* printer Benjamin Edes was another of the Nine, and Paul knew him from the business he conducted with the paper. Paul would come to know several of the others in the coming years as well. All but two were tradesmen like him.[13]

The Nine had a plan; whether Paul played a part is not known, though given his proximity and relationships, it's easy to imagine. What's more, after 1 August, Paul's ledgers show a curious lack of business until 14 September.[14] Not like Paul to go idle. What was he up to during those six weeks?

On 14 August, the mob hanged an effigy of Oliver on a big elm at the south end of town, soon to be infamously and widely known as the Liberty Tree.

By sundown the mob swarmed Oliver's dock at the shoreline, tore down the new building, and then moved to Oliver's house, where they beheaded the effigy in view of the home. Carrying and dragging planks and beams from the demolished structure, they started a fire once they'd arrived at Fort Hill. They torched the effigy, and the protest leaders made speeches before calling it a night. But stragglers had more fun in store.

While the mob torched the effigy on Fort Hill, Oliver and family made a hasty getaway. Just in time. Some of the mob broke away from the fiery festivities and made for Oliver's house. They tore down the fencing, beat their way into the house, and sacked the place. Destroyed furniture. Ripped up the walls. Raided his cellar. Tore down the carriage house, its lumber and that of the demolished fence sent up in flames.

Governor Bernard feared for his safety and boarded a boat for Castle Island, while Hutchinson and the sheriff showed more bravery. They tried to disperse the mob, who sent them scurrying away from the sting of flying stones.

The rioters finally broke up around midnight.[15]

The following day was a flurry. A town meeting was called and condemned the riot and destruction of Oliver's building. It did little else. No arrests were made. A group of men then met with Oliver and told him to expect more of the same, whereupon he resigned his post. That night the mob ankled up Fort Hill and set things ablaze once more. Bernard could see the glow of the flames from his perch at Castle Island.[16]

Whose house was next?

The next night they surrounded Thomas Hutchinson's house. Swarms of eager eyes glinted in the dimming light. Men shifting weight on their legs as they rubbed their hands together. They walked to the door and started pounding, calling for Hutchinson. He hid indoors, but a friend persuaded the pack that their quarry had already fled, and the mob dispersed. Hutchinson let out a sigh of relief. He should have held his breath.[17]

In stepped Paul's old friend, Rev. Jonathan Mayhew. Fresh from public battle over the imposition of an American bishopric, he now announced his opposition to the Stamp Act and fought against this political imposition with equal ferocity. The law could only be enforced, he said, "at the point of a sword," and "no people are under religious obligation to be slaves. . . ."[18] He alerted friends that he would address the matter in a sermon. The text: two verses from the fifth chapter of St. Paul's letter to the Galatians. It was a stemwinder.

Sunday, 25 August, Mayhew ascended the pulpit in his silver wig, flowing black robes, and stiff white neck bands. His finger traced down the page of the open Bible to verses 12 and 13. He read, "I would they were even"—imagine his hand coming down in a chopping motion—"cut off which trouble you. For, brethren, ye have been called unto liberty. . . ."[19]

The next day started with a bonfire. Not a good sign. Horns blasted; drums thumped; voices shouted. The mob spilled out of doors, gathered, and swelled again. The first house upon which they descended was that of customs man Charles Paxton. They pelted the place with stones, bricks, and whatever else was quick to hand. The owner of the house finally emerged and quelled the mob by giving the rioters a barrel of punch. Worked for him, but liquoring a mob is probably not the best course of action.[20] They were only just getting started.

They next swarmed the houses of two others connected to customs enforcement, William Story, the registrar of the

A Stamp Act mob in action.
Library of Congress.

Admiralty, and Comptroller Benjamin Hallowell.[21] They destroyed the dwellings. Next, Hutchinson's.

Hutchinson and family poured out the back of the house. Through the front doors burst the mob. The invaders spread through the house, destroying or stealing everything within reach. They ripped paintings off the walls, battered furniture to splinters, tore down wainscoting, and knocked over interior walls. They pilfered clothes, plates, and £900 in cash. They raided his wine cellar and destroyed his library, pitching into the mud all of his books and papers. They tore up the garden, snapped the trees, and leveled the fence. And the house—they tried tearing it down too. They worked for hours at it, finally pulling down the cupola atop the house. The damage was astounding, amounting to more than £2,000.[22]

Hutchinson later heard testimony from some of the riot participants. One man threw the cause back at Mayhew; the rioter, as Hutchinson later wrote, was "excited" to the destruction "by this sermon . . . he thought he was doing God['s] service."[23] I suppose that this and others of Mayhew's hearers failed to note the end of verse 13: "[O]nly use not liberty for an occasion to the flesh, but by love serve one another." Several of Mayhew's leading parishioners said he didn't stress that part of the text.[24]

Mayhew disclaimed any responsibility.

Bernard noted that Paxton, Story, and Hallowell had all been targeted because of their links to the government's antismuggling efforts. Same with Hutchinson. In a letter about the riots, Bernard said Hutchinson was targeted as chief justice, "as it was in that Character he suffered; for this connecting him with the Admiralty & Custom house was occasioned by his granting writs of assistance to the Custom house officers, upon Accession of his present Majesty; which was so strongly opposed by the Merchants that the Arguments in Court from the Bar and upon the Bench lasted three days. The Chief Justice took the lead in granting the writs, and now he has paid for it."[25]

Patriot leaders were startled by the violence of the riot and purposed to keep a tighter rein on the rowdier element—to whatever extent they could.

The Loyal Nine had originally formed to rebuff the Stamp Act. It morphed into the Sons of Liberty. Other outfits in New York, Connecticut, and elsewhere were already using the name.

Using various stunts and theatrics, the Sons of Liberty continued through the winter and spring of 1766 the protests begun by the Loyal Nine in the summer of 1765.

One tactic involved Paul's skills as a copperplate engraver. Instead of hymnbooks and hemp mills, this time he etched plates for his first political cartoon. He pinched the design from a British cartoonist. Among other things, Revere's image shows men representing the united colonists in opposing a winged dragon. The man at the forefront of the colonists represents Boston. He has one hand on a sword as the other wrests a copy of the Magna Charta from the clutches of the dragon—representing the fight over taxation without representation.[26]

In January 1766 the *Boston Gazette* announced the print for sale. The revolution would be advertised, which was good because Paul needed the money. Take-home in 1765 was only £60, and in the fall, Revere proved Poor

The flamboyant John Hancock.
Library of Congress.

Richard's adage that lenders have better memories than debtors; a merchant attached his estate for a £10 debt stemming from a loan he took out two and a half years before (when money wasn't great but was better than it was in 1765).[27]

The Sons of Liberty had better political victories than financial. While leaders from the several colonies met together for the official Stamp Act Congress and asserted the right to no taxation without representation, the Sons led boycotts of British goods, called *nonimportation*, and they staged mock trials against the stamp paper from Britain. Their more eloquent members penned acidic squibs in newspapers like the *Boston Gazette* against the government. The tactics worked. Patriots won an upset in the May elections to the General Court. The *Gazette* demonized thirty-two representatives as "Tools of the Governor." Nearly two-thirds of them were ousted. In their place slid radical men like Otis and Adams, and up-and-comers like John Hancock.[28]

CHAPTER 9

Parties

*In which the end of the Stamp Act is celebrated
by great and common alike, before Paul bends his
back in his trade again and all merrymaking is
cut short by a grievous and untimely death.*

The Stamp Act was supposed to go into effect in
November 1765. Because of the sharp and organized resistance by patriots in Massachusetts and the other
colonies, it never did. But neither did it officially go away.
Tensions were high as the crisis remained unresolved.

Life went on. Sometimes in ways good—Frances Revere
was born 19 February 1766 and baptized just four days
later.[1]

And other times in ways bad—including the aggravation
of a sore Masonic nerve. Here's what happened: a jagged

rift had divided Masons in England over revision of rules and rituals. Two camps emerged, Ancients and Moderns, and the division was deep enough that it persisted across the pond. Because the boys who started Revere's lodge, St. Andrew's, numbered themselves with the Ancients, the Moderns at St. John's Grand Lodge, which received its charter first, denied them proper fellowship. Revere and others at St. Andrew's were offended and sought to mend the rift—at least as far as Boston was concerned. At first the efforts were rebuffed and the rift worsened. St. John's suggested St. Andrew's members were only "irregular masons" at best. But then by May, things cooled. A meeting on 2 May found some measure of amelioration. Yet like the Stamp Act crisis, the matter was left unresolved.[2]

Other things looked more promising than healing old wounds. Paul was still getting job orders, even if they were fewer than desired. On 16 May, for instance, he got an order for a silver snuff box for fellow Mason and North End artisan Adam Colson. Not that he had much time to get started on it.

That same day, a Friday, the brigantine *Harrison* slid into wharf, and Captain Shubael Coffin unloaded news more valued than any other incoming freight: Parliament had repealed the Stamp Act. Celebration was immediate. On Saturday church bells rang, guns sounded, music echoed, ships unfurled their banners, and labors commenced on a blowout for Monday. Revere and the Sons of Liberty worked up an oiled-paper obelisk for the party, decorated top to bottom on all four sides with portraiture, inscriptions, and scenes depicting the events of the Stamp Act struggle. (Shouts and huzzahs. Roaring bonfires. Imagine the distraction as Revere and the others hurried to finish the design.)[3]

Three of four scenes depict America as an Indian chief with a feather headdress, a long bow, and a quiver full of arrows. In the first image, he lies despondent beneath a pine and menaced by the prime minister, an Anglican bishop, and a bat-winged demon clutching a copy of the Stamp Act. Liberty, pictured as a goddess, hovers above America, and toplofty doggerel implores her:

> O thou, whom next to Heav'n we most revere,
> Fair LIBERTY! Thou lovely Goddess, hear!
> Have we not woo'd thee, won thee, held thee long,
> Lain in thy Lap & melted on thy Tongue.
> Thro Death & Dangers rugged paths pursu'd
> And led thee smiling to this SOLITUDE.
> Hid thee within our Hearts most golden Cell
> And brav'd the Powers of Earth & the Powers of Hell.
> GODDESS! We cannot part, thou must not fly;
> Be SLAVES! We dare to Scorn it—dare to die.

But the lives of America's colonists are not required. Help comes, and America next bows before a group of rescuers while the persecutors are driven back and lightning strikes over their heads. Then, beneath this inscription—

Our FAITH approved, our LIBERTY restor'd,
Our Hearts bend grateful to our Sover'gn Lord

—the final scene shows King George III introducing America to the goddess Liberty, now on foot and approaching.[4] Colonists generally thought of Parliament as housing their foes; they considered King George a friend and benefactor. There was plenty of time and opportunity to adjust that opinion. But first, revelry!

It started in the wee hours of Monday morning. The bells rang in one church after another, cranking away on the bronze chimes until the entire town reverberated and pulsed with the peals. Then the cannons at Castle Island and the batteries ripped through the air, pounding and booming and blowing to pieces any hopes of quiet. Into the still-dark streets minstrels sent strains of flute and flights of fiddle and thumps of drums. Then ships in the harbor met the rosy dawn with cannon fire, and guns throughout town answered with staccato pops and cracks. Buildings, ships, and steeples flew flags, banners, and streamers; the Liberty Tree—the elm upon which Oliver's effigy had hung the prior year—flapped and fluttered from crest to rootstock.[5]

By dusk the Sons of Liberty had the obelisk ready on the Common. They planned to move it to the Liberty Tree later in the celebration. No one had ever seen such a thing. Some 280 lamps were lit within it, radiating an amber glow. It was breathtaking.[6]

Then, as night rushed in, the fireworks came out. Rockets

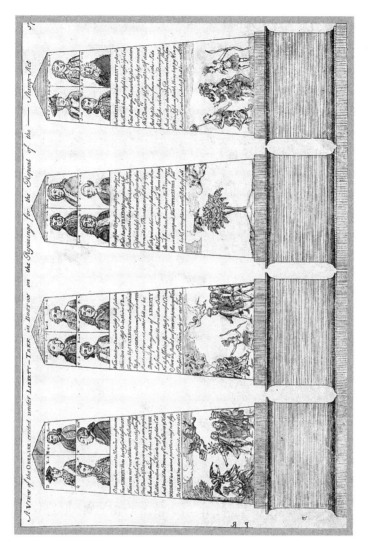

Paul Revere's engraving of the illuminated obelisk.
Library of Congress.

sent curling smoke and sparks through the air in serpentine arcs and loops, cracking, bursting, exploding in the night. Saltpeter, brimstone, and charcoal fumes suffused the air as smoke drifted across the Common. No one minded. There were music and feasting and drinking. Money was raised, and the jailed were freed. John Hancock set the Madeira flowing free in front of his house—more than a barrelful—where still more rockets were fired. With just an hour left in the day, a fireworks wheel mounted on the top of the obelisk was lit—a spinning, sparkling display followed by one even more impressive. Streams of rockets were launched in fiery gusts, sent whizzing and whirring into the upturned spangled bowl of the sky.[7]

Revere engraved a copper plate of the obelisk, the only thing that survived of it. In the flower of all those sparks and flames it's a wonder it didn't catch fire sooner, but finally an hour after midnight, twenty-four hours after the celebration started, the obelisk burst into flames and burned to nothing.[8]

It wasn't just celebrants who observed the Stamp Act's repeal. A few days later, Rev. Jonathan Mayhew climbed into his pulpit at West Church and homilized on a passage from the Psalms: "Our soul is escaped as a bird out of the snare of the fowlers: the snare is broken, and we are escaped." His last sermon on the Stamp Act unleashed fury like something from the book of Revelation. What would happen this time?

The language was strong enough—he called the imposition of the tax an "execrable design!"—but he held the gate on the Apocalypse. No armies. No plagues. No horsemen. Mayhew's delivery was marked more by ebullience, thanksgiving, and even an attempt to rebuild trust between the colonies and Britain and, like Revere's doggerel, between the people and their king.

Mayhew was determined to help his listeners pluck a bloom from the bramble. Alluding to the story of Joseph's bondage in Egypt, he noted that God redeems the evil machinations of men for purposes of his own. One example: "The great shock which was lately given to our liberties, may end in the confirmation and enlargement of them: As it is said, the stately oaks of the forest take the deeper root, extend their arms the farther, and exalt their venerable heads the higher for being agitated by storms and tempests." And another: "Almighty God . . . in whose hands are the hearts of all men, not excepting those of kings . . . hath inspired the people of America with a noble spirit of liberty, and remarkably united them in standing up for that invaluable blessing."

So the snare was broken, the people delivered. Now what? Mayhew might not have been a Puritan in doctrine, but he was one in culture. The people's obsession over the Stamp Act crisis produced "a great neglect and stagnation of business." So Mayhew told his people to get to work: "Let us all apply ourselves with diligence, and in the fear of God, to the duties respective of our stations." Laborers "have had so much to say about government and politics, in the late times of danger, tumult, and confusion, that many of them seemed to forget [that] they had anything to do. . . ." Mayhew implored his people to "do something more, and talk something less. . . ."[9]

Better get back to that snuff box, Paul.

Revere put his back into it. It wasn't just Colson's snuff box. His business picked up in the month following the Stamp Act celebration. It was as if customers felt free to spend, free to buy. They shook off the gloom and hesitation that held them, and in the gush of excitement and joviality, they walked into Revere's shop and ordered, ordered, ordered: everything from spoons and tankards to coffeepots and gold brooches.[10]

But despite the admonition of the preacher, Revere and the rest of the town kept talking. In the years following the Stamp Act protests, Revere made his presence evermore present in a growing number of politically charged clubs, including the Merchant Club, the Long Room Club, the North End Caucus, and others. In their late-night sessions, talk about the rights of Englishmen and natural liberties flowed as easily as the rum and Madeira. Many of the men in these clubs were merchants and lawyers—gentlemen—making Revere a little outclassed. But biographer Esther Forbes claimed that he was welcomed because of his ease at moving between worlds, communicating the ideas of Boston's radical Whig faction with the day laborers and mechanics of Boston's North End.

Boston had always been run by a network of activists

who met in clubs. The clubs met in private to do what they would do in public through organizations like the Sons of Liberty. More and more, communication between the various groups and interests in the colonies seemed necessary. The point hit home to Mayhew while lying in bed early Sunday morning.

Massachusetts churches were congregational. There was no bishop or even presbytery to govern the individual churches. If a local church couldn't answer a question or solve a problem, there was no higher authority to which a buck could pass. They often worked things out by calling other local churches to sit in council. The visiting ministers would listen to testimony and render a nonbinding opinion. Mayhew had in fact been called to just such a council and would be leaving for it the following day.

As he thought about what lay ahead, he realized that this was a model for the colonies. Mayhew figured that if you could bring together decentralized religious bodies, why not decentralized political bodies? He jumped out of bed and scribbled a letter to James Otis, recommending a committee between the colonies patterned after the Stamp Act Congress, when representatives from the disunited colonies came together to offer a unified voice on the tax. The idea was to keep alive the communication between the various colonies.[11] He wanted to preserve that hard-won unity.

"Would it not be very proper & decorous for our assembly to send circular congratulatory Letters to all of the rest without exception, on the repeal, and the present favorable aspect of Things?" The letters would express affection for the mother country and loyalty to the king, and intimate "a desire to cement & perpetuate union among ourselves, by all practical and laudable methods." After all, "for what may be hereafter we cannot tell, however favorable soever the present appearances may be."[12] In other words, let's not let our guard down. Mayhew sent the letter and then hit the road on Monday, 9 June, for his confab.

The council was called to sort out accusations about a local pastor. Testimony started Tuesday, and it was a grueling affair that lasted more than a week. Mayhew played secretary for the proceedings. By 18 June, the council was finished, and so was Mayhew. He left for Boston, physically drained. The weather didn't help. Rain fell through the hot air as he rode. At last, fevered and ill, he crossed Boston Neck.

Over the next few days headaches pummeled him, and by the fourth day after arriving back home, he suffered what was probably a stroke. He faded fast. Local clergy called for a day of prayer. Some concerned about his heterodox views on the Trinity sent someone to speak with him. Not much was said, but the visitor came away saying, "I believe he loves the Lord Jesus Christ, the son of God, sincerely." Mayhew gave up the ghost on 9 July 1766.[13]

Two days later people swarmed to his simple funeral. Fifty-seven carriages and innumerable men and women accompanied the remains. Despite ninety-degree heat, tears for the departed probably ran more than the sweat.[14] It's impossible to imagine Revere anywhere else but in the crowd, and he probably heard the eulogy: "friend to liberty both civil and religious."

To stave off any fading of the reverend's memory, Revere cut an etching of Mayhew. He followed another engraving that was published by old family friend Nathaniel Hurd. Paul's creation is not thought a flattering likeness, and there's scant evidence his portrait was widely published, if published at all. It might have been cut for more personal reasons.[15] Perhaps the same mix of grief and admiration that produced a string of funeral discourses and elegies by both fellow ministers and laity, like the poetic Dr. Benjamin Church.[16]

Mayhew's sermon "The Snare Broken" was published shortly after his death. This from the benediction: "May that God, in whom our help has been, continue to protect us, our rights and privileges! May he direct our paths thro' this uncertain life, and all the changes of it; and of his infinite mercy in Jesus Christ, finally bring us all to those peaceful and glorious regions, where no evil spirits, no wicked flowers will come; where no snares will be spread for us. . . ."[17]

The grandiloquent Dr. Church.
History Picks.

If Mayhew was correct that he was no heretic, then he was already in those glorious regions. As for friends left behind, there were still many snares ahead.

For starters, on 27 July, customs man Charles Paxton set sail for England, planning to advise the government on more effective application of the Navigation Acts.[18]

CHAPTER 10

Boycotts

*In which the confrontations between the king's
customs men and the people of Boston, including
our hero, increase and intensify,
while nonimportation is tried and the
case against taxation is made.*

D espite early indications, Revere and Flagg must have
had some measure of success with their hymnbook
because by the fall of 1766, they were at it again. For this
volume Paul only engraved the plates; Flagg shouldered the
rest of the burden. Titled *Sixteen Anthems*, the new book
featured a Christmas hymn:

Born of a maid, a Virgin pure
Born without Sin, from guilt secure[1]

Mary was no doubt pure, and Christ surely sinless, but Boston's customs agents would never entertain such thoughts about their tax-evading neighbors.

Ebenezer Richardson snitched for a living. So it was no surprise that he told authorities they could find smuggled spirits at the home of Captain Daniel Malcolm. On the morning of 24 September 1766, two customs officials, William Sheafe and Benjamin Hallowell (whose house had been destroyed in last year's riots), showed up for a look-see. Malcolm gave them the tour. Showed them this room, then that. Showed them every room but one.

So what was inside there?

Malcolm, refusing to open the door, said that he rented the room and couldn't just pop in. Hallowell and Sheafe were insistent, Malcolm undeterred. Finally Hallowell and Sheafe brought in the renter, but he wasn't playing along either and claimed he didn't have the key. Things got testy. Hallowell and Sheafe demanded that Malcolm spring the door. But he, armed with a sword and pair of pistols, said nothing doing. If anyone so much as tried, he'd "blow his Brains out." This wasn't going well, so after a good deal of back and forth, Hallowell and Sheafe left to get help.[2]

Later they arrived with Sheriff Greenleaf and two more officials. By now, word spread what was going down, and a crowd gathered outside Malcolm's home while the authorities tried to get back inside. No luck. Malcolm barricaded himself indoors.

Paul heard what was happening and joined the growing crowd. He testified that one of the customs officials there appeared "very angry." But the crowd—some two hundred strong—was the picture of "decency and good order."[3] Another witness said the mob was so solemn and sober that the people might as well have been gathered to hear George Whitefield preach, which was a little ironic considering that Whitefield had actually sermonized against smuggling.[4]

While the people were amassed, the officials couldn't enter the house for fear of a riot. And the mob showed no sign of leaving until the threat to Malcolm's property passed. After an hour Paul quit the standoff—maybe Mayhew's encouragement to get back to work still resonated with him—but the mob persisted till nightfall when the authorities finally decided against pushing any further action. They retired to pen a report, and Malcolm rewarded his guardian angels with wine by the bucketful, some of it probably smuggled.[5]

Bernard had depositions taken and sent them along to Britain. They could only help prove whatever Charles Paxton was busy telling people there.

In October, Sam Adams, James Otis, and other patriot leaders finally laid eyes on the depositions and were scandalized. They were, said Adams, "a partial Account" and contained testimony from disreputable people such as Richardson. "This Fellow has for a long time subsisted by the Business of an Informer & is said to be such an one as was never encouraged under any Administration but such as those [of] Nero or Caligula—that the Evidence of this detestable Person might have its Weight, they gave him the Addition of Esquire."[6] They took nineteen of their own depositions, among them one from Revere.

The town meeting sent the Bernard depositions and its own to their London agent in hopes of setting straight the record and preventing the one-sided account from libeling them before the Crown.

Despite the efforts of Adams and Otis, the only message resonating in Britain was that things in Boston were getting rowdy and required additional attention.

It wasn't just the mobs that attracted Britain's attention. After repeal of the Stamp Act, Parliament was up Debt Creek without a farthing. In stepped "Champagne Charlie" Townshend, chancellor of the Exchequer, with a proposal that was surely concocted during one of his famous benders.

In late spring 1767 he put forward several acts that he claimed would raise revenues, reassert Parliament's authority over the colonies, and improve customs collections. For starters, he called for new duties on glass, pigments, paper, and tea. Historian G. B. Warden points out that the last two were really meant as barbs. Stamp Act protesters opposed tax stamps printed on *some* paper. Townshend thumbed his nose in return by taxing *all* paper. As for tea, Townshend arranged to cut its cost by reimbursements and thus reduce the need to smuggle Dutch tea despite the new levies. By these two measures Parliament symbolically reasserted its right to tax and practically reinforced the Navigation Acts.[7] The acts also created a new American board of customs commissioners, on which Paxton would serve, thanks to Townshend.[8]

For the majority of Brits, Townshend's plan seemed sober enough. If Americans benefited from British protection, they should shoulder the burden. The minority opinion was concerned that if the Americans were paying for protection, they couldn't pay for British goods.[9] Neither opinion factored the American concern about the propriety of taxing Americans at all—the whole taxation without representation issue hadn't changed but was just as ignored as before.

The last time the colonists felt ignored, they went on a rampage. So in August 1767, Hutchinson sent out what must have been an oblique message to potential rioters that if a man's home or property was threatened and he happened to kill someone in its defense, he was guilty of no more than manslaughter. Striking back against the rioters no longer carried the risk of a murder charge. Hutchinson was clearly worried about the same sort of tumult that surrounded the Stamp Act.[10]

But violence wasn't the first response of the colonists. They first responded by repeating a tactic they lightly employed during the Stamp Act: nonimportation. From the 31 August 1767 *Boston Gazette*: "To what alas! Is

America reduced[?] This land for which our fathers fought and bled, must now become the den of slavery." If the British figured they could get away with taxes because the colonists required the goods, the boycott was vital to show Parliament that they could "freely part with the gay trappings of a butterfly."[11]

On 28 October the town meeting deliberated in Faneuil Hall about the proper response. James Otis moderated. The town decided on nonimportation and enumerated the boycotted goods. The list included everything from sugar and mustard and snuff, to ready-made clothing and shoes and furs. Clocks, cheese, glue, and gold buttons were banned. So were muffs, gloves, and hats. And forget about cordage, deck nails, and fire engines while you're at it. The litany, unorganized in any obvious fashion, included much more than gay trappings. It was a rambling assortment of goods, common and fine—many of which the consumerist and commercialist Americans would have some trouble living without.[12]

In crafting the boycott, they also reaffirmed that nonviolence would pair with nonimportation. In the same town meeting that approved the boycott, Otis drilled this point, even going so far as to remind the assembly that during the reign of Charles I "our forefathers . . . for fifteen years . . . were continually offering up prayers to their God, and petitions to their king, for redress of grievances, before they would betake themselves to any forcible measures. . . ."[13]

The new commissioners arrived about a week later on 5 November. It was rainy, but that didn't stop the hecklers

Patriots tarring and feathering a tax man.
Library of Congress.

from greeting them at the docks with an effigy of the devil, tagged "Charles"—Townshend or Paxton? Six of one, half a dozen of the other—and another labeled "Everybody's Humble Servant & Nobody's Friend." Must have been Paxton. They followed him, chanting, "Liberty, Property, and no Commissioners."[14]

But nothing worse than a ribbing occurred.

"Let the persons and properties of our most inveterate enemies be safe," penned Joseph Warren for the *Gazette* after the arrival of Paxton and company. "Let not a hair of their scalps be touched. Let this be the language of all—no mobs, no confusions, no tumults."[15]

Against persons the patriots would for now be restrained. Not so against policies. Against these the patriots were only getting started.

After pulling a deft parliamentary procedure on 11 February 1768—that is, waiting till his opponents left town on recess—Samuel Adams pushed a "circular letter" through the General Court.[16] The letter, sent to the other colonial legislatures, encouraged them to "harmonize with each other" on the subject of Parliament's tax schemes.[17] Adams constructed a simple and watertight case, both echoing and advancing the arguments from the Stamp Act crisis:

- Parliament's power comes from the British Constitution;
- it cannot violate the constitution's own provisions "without destroying its own foundation";
- the constitution "limits both Sovereignty and allegiance";
- the colonies "have an equitable Claim to the full enjoym[en]t of the fundamental Rules of the British Constitution";
- the constitution enshrines a natural right to property, "that what a man has honorably acquir[e]d is absolutely his own" and "cannot be taken from him without his consent";

- the colonies can legitimately assert this "natural and constitutional Right";
- the Townshend Acts are "Infringements of their natural & constitutional Rights" because the colonies are unrepresented in Parliament;
- real representation is an "utter Impracticability," given cost, distance, etc.;
- ergo, there's no way for Parliament to legally raise taxes in America.[18]

After leaving no room for the British authorities to either wiggle or wangle, Adams still concluded by expressing "firm Confidence in the King" to right these wrongs, while crying foul about "Enemys of the Colonys" smearing them before Parliament "as factious disloyal & having a disposition to make themselves independent of the Mother Country."[19] He didn't name Bernard, Hutchinson, and Paxton, but there can be little doubt about the sort he included on his enemies' list.

The feeling was mutual. Not a month went by when the patriots didn't, in the minds of Bernard and company, confirm the need for London to send troops.

In March, for instance, Bostonians gathered to celebrate the repeal of the Stamp Act. While the original news had reached the colonies in May 1766, the official date of repeal was 18 March, and on that day in 1768, Bostonians relived their victory. Amid the barking guns and the booming drums, countless townsfolk, both patriot and loyalist, turned out to see the fluttering banners and hear the soaring orations.[20]

Adams and the patriot leaders kept the anarchic antics to a minimum, but celebrants nonetheless set two effigies dangling from the boughs of the Liberty Tree, one of Paxton and another of the inspector general. As day turned into night, some eight hundred men mobbed together and shouted in parade past Bernard's mansion and then surrounded both Paxton's and the inspector general's houses. Nothing much happened, but in the slow-moving hours that the mass circled and menaced, the residents could be forgiven the feeling that they might at any minute be swarmed, rushed, and torn limb from limb.[21]

With mobs in the streets—even "peaceful" ones—the public declarations about nonviolence failed to soothe the jangled nerves. In the fall of 1767 and early months of 1768, commissioners like Paxton and officials like Bernard and Hutchinson scribbled a series of letters and sent them to London. Subject: Boston's slow-boil anarchy and the need for troops to clamp down the lid before it bubbled over.[22] The supplicants sometimes masked their requests. Bernard, for instance, feared what the patriots might do if he asked outright for troops.[23] Even his nonrequests communicated the situation plainly enough. The events of 18 March only validated the earlier letters and gave cause for new ones.

Out the door flew a new blast of salvos and petitions: send help!

Easy odds to say Revere was part of the excitement—though even easier to excuse him if his participation was minimal. He had other reasons to celebrate. The day after the festivities, the Reveres welcomed into the world the family's newest member, Mary.[24] (It was common to re-employ names when an earlier bearer had died.)

Later that month the littlest Revere was baptized, but not at the Cockerel. The flock's new pastor, Ebenezer Pemberton, identified too closely with the loyalists and the church's leading member, Thomas Hutchinson.[25] Benjamin Church, regularly given to flights of poetry, lampooned the both of them in verse:

> There's puffing Pem [Pemberton], who does condemn
> All Freedom's noble sons,
> And Andrew Sly, who oft draws nigh
> To Tommy skin and bones [Hutchinson].[26]

In a time when the politics so sharply divided, it's none too surprising that Revere withdrew from the fellowship and worshipped among more like-minded congregants. Mary received the sacrament at West Church. With Mayhew gone, the new pastor, Simeon Howard, steered the church in the radical politics and theology that separated many of the patriot leaders from the establishment loyalists.[27]

But a new mouth to feed presented new complications along with the joys. Paul booked less income in 1767 than at any other time before in business—not even £48.[28] And while orders started strong at the beginning of 1768, Paul wasn't turning down business even if that meant working with loyalists. He'd always done so. He was friendly and open and usually separated his politics from his profession. But the month before Mary was born, he even cut printing plates for John Mein, a loyalist publisher who only weeks before had caned John Gill, Revere's friend and printer of the *Boston Gazette*.[29] Mein felt he'd been slandered by the paper. All parties must have understood that business was business, however, because afterward Revere still continued to work with both Mein and Gill and even charged jobs to both men on the same calendar day.[30]

Tolerant of his customers and expansive of his services, Paul not only did business with almost anyone, but he was also quick to learn a new means for separating fellow citizens from their cash, including dentistry. Revere's friend Joshua Brackett lodged a surgeon from England who not only practiced the trade but taught Paul. Soon enough Paul was advertising in the *Boston Gazette* that anyone

> so unfortunate as to lose their Fore-Teeth by Accident, or otherways . . . may have them re-placed with artificial Ones, that looks as well as the Natural, & answers the End of Speaking to all Intents, by PAUL REVERE, Goldsmith, near the Head of Dr. Clarke's Wharf, Boston.[31]

And one of Paul's customers? His old friend and fellow Mason, Joseph Warren.

In addition to taking what business he could, Paul seemed to have taken whatever payment he could. Paul made picture frames for famed portraitist John Singleton Copley

A young Paul Revere by the able hand of portraitist
John Singleton Copley.
Getty Images.

and sat for his own portrait to even the books.[32] He certainly couldn't have justified spending the outrageous sum such a painting would otherwise cost. Other of Copley's subjects could afford it. Not Revere. Even if you didn't know about his finances, you could see it plainly enough. Copley's subjects wore elaborate garments made from the finest fabrics. Paul, while wearing a fine vest with gold buttons, nonetheless sat in his rough linen shirt at his workbench, tools at the ready and holding a gleaming teapot.

No aristocrat's distant gaze, just the immediate piercing eyes.[33] There's a bit of the same intensity in Copley's portrait of Samuel Adams, who also dressed plainly for his portrait, but Revere's eyes have a special intensity.[34] In the time of boycotts and long laundry lists of banned goods, austerity, frugality, and industry were the images to portray—if not only for rank necessity. In 1768 Revere didn't have to work too hard at looking austere; it came naturally.

But while he'd work for all comers, the lines that had been drawn between patriot and loyalist were about to get sharper, wider, and deeper.

John Hancock got crosswise with the customs commissioners in April of '68. His ship *Lydia*—a ship his uncle Thomas had used to smuggle goods—landed, and while it was at dock a customs agent began snooping around under deck at night. The crew caught him, roughed him up, and then turned him loose. Hancock answered to the court for the treatment of the man and was exonerated because the man was acting outside the law.

Officials kept an eye on Hancock, and when his ship *Liberty* docked in May, they were certain he'd smuggled wine from the cargo. He'd only reported a small number of barrels, and yet his captain was so wearied from unloading that he died of exhaustion. That didn't jibe. Officials suspected that the crew offloaded vastly more than the reported amount but couldn't get any information. They itched to act. Warren warned customs man Benjamin Hallowell that if they tried to seize the vessel, "there would be a great Uproar."[35]

Then came June. And then came the *Romney*, a British naval vessel. Emboldened by the nearby guns of the *Romney*, informers soon surfaced to tell all about smuggled wine from the *Liberty*. Customs men could finally act, Warren's prediction be hanged.

As the skies darkened on 10 June, Hallowell and two others made for the wharf and formally seized the ship. People assembled by twos, tens, hundreds, then finally a mob of nearly a thousand men. As the *Romney* swooped in on the *Liberty*, the mob chucked stones at the sailors, who quickly lashed the ships together and moved them back into the bay away from the wharf. Someone ran and told Hancock what was happening, but he stayed out of it.[36] He probably knew what was coming.

As the officials left the wharf, they were assaulted by flying stones, sticks, and debris. The men ran but were overtaken. The mob grabbed one and pulled him through an open sewer before he freed himself and escaped down an alley. Another was dragged by the hair over the cobbled street until rescued. Hallowell was battered, bloodied, and discarded in a heap.

Around the homes of the commissioners swarmed the mob, sending rocks through windowpanes, shattering the glass into clinking, crashing shards. Bands of men skulked through the streets with torches fluttering and blazing, looking for customs officials to terrorize. They dragged a pleasure boat owned by one of the commissioners from the water's edge, hauled the vessel up to the Common, and set it afire. Patriot leaders intervened and dispersed the crowd, but the damage was done.

All but one of the commissioners escaped the following day to Castle Island, and a new string of pleas and petitions made their way to London.[37]

But the requests were unnecessary. Things were already in motion.

CHAPTER 11

Showdown

*In which the patriots count themselves in the
camp of radicals and the Crown responds by
military imposition before Governor Bernard
is knighted and his chapter closed.*

London ran even shorter on patience than it did on revenues. The British government, through Bernard, ordered the Massachusetts General Court to rescind the February circular letter that Adams had sent out to all the other colonies in opposition to Britain's claim of taxing authority. Suddenly now faced with a direct challenge to its own provincial sovereignty, and galvanized by Adams, the General Court told Bernard where he could put the order. After several days of hot-winded debate, during which colonial legislators called the king's ministers "ignorant, ill-educated, francophiliac despots," the vote came down against Bernard, 92–17.[1]

That was at the end of June 1768. On 1 July Bernard answered by dissolving the General Court. The patriots answered Bernard by hoisting glasses to toast the "Glorious Ninety-two." They had other designs on the scurrilous seventeen.

For his part Paul went to work etching a cartoon of two demons using pitchforks to prod the seventeen into the fiery maw of a jagged-toothed dragon. The seventeen trudge onward as the first demon says, "Now I've got you, a fine hawl by Jove." Revere cut each figure alike, all in their buckled shoes, overcoats, and tricornered hats. Only Dr. John Calef stands out. Playing on the pronunciation of his last name, Paul gave him a cow's head. He patterned and titled the piece after an earlier etching from England—"A Warm Place—Hell."[2]

As Revere worked on the plate in his shop, scratching his lines and cutting his crosshatches, in stepped Benjamin Church. He looked over the design—the demons, the monster, the reluctant rescinders. The Muses coughed, and Church added a flourish of verse below the depiction. Here's part:

On brave RESCINDERS! To yon yawning cell
SEVENTEEN such miscreants sure will startle Hell
There puny Villains d—n'd for petty sin
On such distinguish'd SCOUNDRELS gaze and grin[3]

Not the most electrifying lines, no, but decades later, Revere could still rattle them off from memory.[4]

Edes and Gill inked the presses and published the cartoon on a broadside with more doggerel and a list of the rescinders—"The Seventeen Proselytes to his E[nem]y's Doctrinal Faith of Submission!"—complete with mock titles for each, including, "His E[nem]y's Interpreters of hard Sayings," "His E[nem]y's chief Soothsayer, and grand Oracle of Infallibility," and "His E[nem]y's Inspector of the Fiery Furnace."[5]

But Paul did more than attack the rescinders; he also saluted the Ninety-two. Fifteen Sons of Liberty, among them Captain Daniel Malcolm, commissioned him to craft a silver punch bowl to honor the nonrescinders. It weighed just shy of 45 ounces of silver and held 45 gills of punch (almost a gallon). The only thing Revere handled with any subtlety on the bowl was his own modest artisan's mark on the underside. The rest was a riot of patriotic inscription, symbols, and scrollwork. On just one side: flags marked "Magna Charta" and "Bill of Rights," a torn sheet of paper labeled "General Warrants" (like the writs of assistance), and a name and number inside a foliated frame—Wilkes and the number (there it is again) 45.[6]

Here's the significance: John Wilkes, a member of Parliament, anonymously produced a radical newspaper called the *North Briton*. He landed in a roiling kettle when both king and Parliament took more than the usual offense at issue No. 45, published in April 1763.[7] Wilkes was arrested, charged with seditious libel, and sent to the Continent in exile. After five years, he returned to England a Promethean figure for his undaunted opposition to government abuse and regained his seat to Parliament.

With their own struggles fresh in mind, a committee of the Boston Sons of Liberty, including Adams and Otis, commenced correspondence with Wilkes in the summer of 1768. "That the British constitution still exists is our glory," they wrote; "feeble and infirm as it is, we cannot we will not despair of it. . . . Your perseverance in the good old cause may still prevent the great system from dashing to pieces." Along with some patriot literature, they sent a pair of turtles, prized for soup making: one weighed 45 pounds, the other 47. Together they summed 92.[8]

Wilkes received the letter but was already back in the stewpot. After his election, he was again arrested.

His supporters rallied, and in May 1768 several thousand massed in London at St. George's Field, near the prison, shouting, "Wilkes and Liberty!" and "D—n the king, d—n the Parliament, d—n the justices!" The mob surrounded the soldiers on guard, shouted at them, and hurled stones. Finally the soldiers leveled their guns, and cracking fire punctuated the taunts. Several people dropped in clumps.

Like seeds cast down in bloody soil, the dead sprang up as thorny brambles all throughout town. "The capital," said Benjamin Franklin, who was then in London, "is now a daily scene of lawless riot and confusion." The tussles and tumults weren't all draped in the toplofty principle over which the Sons of Liberty claimed to agitate. Rioters also busted heads over wages and the price of bread and beer.[9]

Revere and fellow patriots found a hero and martyr in Wilkes, but by London's lights, they'd linked themselves to a criminal and seditionist. Throughout the 1760s disturbances erupted in England. The Wilkes incident in 1768 was merely the most recent and egregious.

The panicky salvos from the commissioners and Bernard convinced London that similar anarchy was under way in America. Before news of the *Liberty* riot reached England—before it had even happened in fact—London had already grown weary of its colonists. And worried. Determined that restoring and upholding Britain's sovereignty required troops, the secretary of state for the Americas signed on 8 June an order commanding General Thomas Gage in New York to send his redcoats to Boston. When news of the 10 June riot finally reached London, it only confirmed the need to send more men.[10]

Revere and the Sons of Liberty were still oblivious to the upcoming troop mobilization when they dined on ninety-two different dishes on 14 August for the annual commemoration of the Stamp Act resistance.[11] But that differed by September, when rumors blew bone-chilling gusts through town. British soldiers had stationed in Boston before—to fight the French. But this time the redcoats were coming to impose the Crown's dominion on its subjects. This time Boston patriots were the enemy. Around every corner and down every street came the word: the king's men were on their way.

Revere and the patriots made fevered preparations. They held meetings. They cranked presses. They even dusted off muskets. But in the end all they could do was await the coming menace.

And then it arrived.

On Friday, 30 September 1768, "the Ships of War, armed Schooners, Transports, &c. Came up the Harbour and Anchored round the Town," recalled Revere—and here was the really unnerving part—"their Cannon loaded, a Spring on their Cables, as for a regular Siege." Ships flanked the town, guns trained on the people. Soon the troops came ashore, boat after boat, till they all stood at Long Wharf, where, said Paul, they "Formed and Marched with insolent Parade, Drums beating, Fifes playing, and Colours flying. . . ."[12]

The drummers wore yellow coats, but most of the troops wore red. They coursed up the dirty ribbon of King Street like a long line of scarlet beads.

Despite talk of armed opposition, Boston gave no resistance. The situation was tense, but for respect, for fear, for self-protection, for whatever amalgam of motives, most people behaved.

Friction was nonetheless unavoidable, and the patriots seized every opportunity to cast the blame. Within days and weeks of the soldiers' arrival, Sam Adams and others started dipping and scribbling, anonymously inking story upon story about soldiers abusing the populace, beating men, assaulting women, and cursing up a storm. Enough of it was true to make an impression—in Boston and in the other colonies.[13]

But the soldiers weren't all frittering away the hours, mugging and molesting and blaspheming. At least not all the time. Yes, they raced horses on the Common during church and sang frivolous songs as they walked by congregations, but little, awkward relationships and alliances formed nonetheless. Some soldiers married Boston girls. Others secured jobs around town to supplement their meager military pay. Some deserted at the leading of the locals. Of those who stuck around, some even participated in local Masonic concerns.

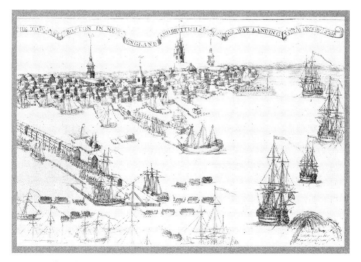

Portion of Paul Revere's engraving of the landing of the troops.
Library of Congress.

The Ancient and Modern Masons still struggled. The dispute cooled through 1766 and much of 1767, but it hadn't been settled. It heated up again in 1768. Revere and the Ancient Masons of St. Andrew's were at a disadvantage, receiving their charter later than St. John's Lodge. More than that, St. John's was a Grand Lodge, meaning it was the direct representative of the Grand Lodge in England. Revere and the others at St. Andrew's considered the need to apply for status as a Grand Lodge—at least then they'd be on equal footing. British troops who were Masons brought their lodge affiliations to Boston, all of them Ancient, just like St. Andrew's. So in November, Revere, Warren, and six others met on the matter with their redcoat Masonic brothers. By December they—patriot Masons and redcoat Masons—were "agreed that it is necessary to have a Grand Master of An[c]ient Masons in America" and further agreed upon officers for the new Grand Lodge. They petitioned their own Grand Lodge back in Scotland.[14]

Revere, Warren, and their fellow Ancients appreciated the support, but whatever Masonic cordiality might mean, Revere knew that American liberty was jeopardized by a standing army and interference by a government in which they had no representation.

In October he etched an image for Edes and Gill to be used in their 1769 almanac. In the lower third of the frame, two women sit. One, America. The other, Britain. Both are holding spears with caps atop. The cap represents liberty.

Paul Revere's engraving, "The Lord God Omnipotent Reigneth."
Library of Congress.

America's has fallen off. Britain's teeters. Behind America, ships are dashed in a storm and crashing against the rocks. But despite the gloomy scenery, hope beams. At the top radiate the words "The LORD GOD Omnipotent reigneth, let the Earth rejoice!" Two angels fly above the darkness.

One says, "Shall not the Lord of all the Earth do Right."[15]
The answer came in just a few months.

Through the newspapers, patriot scribes continued to squib the troops. They warned about the threat to the townsfolk's morals—"The ear being accustomed to oaths and imprecations, will be the less shockt at the profanity, and the frequent spectacles of drunkenness, exhibited in our streets, greatly countenances this shameful and ruinous vice."[16] About the dangers to the fair sex—"Another woman not happening to please some soldier, received a considerable wound on her head with a cutlass; and [another] woman presuming to scream, when laid hold of by a soldier, had a bayonet run through her cheek. . . ."[17] About the need to arm the citizenry—"Instances of the licentious and outrageous behaviour of the *military conservators* of the peace . . . must serve fully to evince that a late vote of this town, calling up on the inhabitants to provide themselves with arms for their defence, was a measure as prudent as it was *legal*. . . ."[18]

But they also used more official channels to address the soldiers' presence in Boston. After Bernard dissolved the General Court the previous summer, the town meeting took on all new importance as the only democratic thing going in Boston—the only official body that would hear and address the concerns of the patriots, primarily because they ran the meeting.

Patriot leaders felt certain that Bernard and Hutchinson

had misrepresented colonial goings-on to London and that those misrepresentations had resulted in the troops. Throughout the winter and early spring of 1769, the patriots met in the town meeting and issued official statement after official statement blasting the "partial or false representations" of "artful and mischievous men."[19] The popular picture now painted Bernard and Hutchinson as the hub of a vast network of government jobholders and hangers-on who gained status and position by slandering the patriots. And then they got proof. Sympathizers in Britain obtained and forwarded six copies of Bernard's letters to patriot leaders on the Governor's Council. They received them 5 April.[20]

The council was outraged by the contents (much of which painted the colonists as lawless and treacherous) and published the letters to let the town get a taste of what Bernard penned about them. The town chewed them over like a pack of terriers. He said what about us?! Bernard's stock dropped like a rock in the bay.[21]

But if the arrival of the letters was like a dart from the devil, something else soon arrived that was a gift from God. Bernard wearied of Boston as much as it did of him; he had been sending requests to leave for months. He finally got an answer on 26 April. According to the letter, the king, while rewarding him with a baronetcy, wanted him to come home and give a report of the colony. Bernard hid the fact of his impending departure. He only revealed the promotion to baronet—for which he was widely mocked.[22]

From the 1 May *Boston Gazette*, directed to Bernard:

YOUR Promotion, Sir, reflects an honor on the Province itself. . . . *Your own* Letters will serve to convince the World, and the latest Posterity, that while you have constantly preserved a sacred and inviolable Regard to punctilious TRUTH, in *every* Representation which you have made of the people . . . you have carefully endeavor'd to give the most *favorable* Colouring to their Conduct and Reputation; And the *Tenderness* which you have ever *remarkably* felt for their *civil* Rights as well as their *Religion*, will not admit of the least Room to question, but that even the Influence you have *evidently* employ'd with Success, to introduce MILITARY Power, and the unwearied Pains you took to get them quarter'd *in the Body of the Town*, sprang from your *Piety* and *Benevolence* of Heart— Pity it is that you have not a PENSION to support your Title. . . . [23]

That last point was surely a dig, knowing the governor's perennial financial troubles. But forget about it. What did he care? Boston wasn't the golden pear he thought it was. It was a pithy apple eaten by worms that plagued him from the moment he'd taken his first bite. Or maybe it was more like a snare. Perhaps he remembered the words of Mayhew's very public sermon and felt the words finally applied to him. The snare was broken, and he was free. He could lameduck his way to the end of his term, 2 August, and then head back to more reasonable shores.[24]

Not so fast.

The patriots made it hard on him. Bernard was compelled by the colonial charter to reconvene the General Court—it had to meet once a year. The patriots dominated the General Court and through it agitated immediately for the removal of the troops. Bernard responded by removing the General Court to Cambridge away from the tumults of Boston. But business in Cambridge was just as sticky, and the court, unable to get Bernard to act the way it desired, fired off a letter to the king himself asking him to fire Bernard. Calling his government "repugnant not only to your Majesty's service, and the welfare of your subjects in the Colony, but even to the first principles of the *British* Constitution," they listed sixteen charges "and many more that might be enumerated," before summing up: "[H]e has rendered his Administration odious to the whole body of the people. . . ."[25]

Then Bernard—in what must have been one of the great you-can't-fire-me-I-quit moments in history—announced that the king had already requested his presence in London.[26]

Finally, Bernard was going.

And the troops as well. While the friction with the soldiers was intense, there had been no more riots since their arrival. Commanders wondered why they were stuck in Boston and ardently petitioned to leave. The only trouble facing the troops, it seemed, was instigated by the troops' very presence. It was time to leave.[27] Four regiments garrisoned in town then. While Bernard tiffed with the court, General Gage ordered away two of the regiments. They started shipping out the first week of July.[28]

Defeated and scorned, Bernard boarded a boat on 31 July. The following day, the ship slipped from the wharf and took its cargo far away.

The town gave him a tremendous send-off. Revere would have seen it all. Guns were fired from his front yard, right there on Clark's Wharf. Bells clanged from church towers, and flags hung from Liberty Tree. Finally at night, the celebrants lit the dark skies with huge bonfires at King Street and on Fort Hill. Bernard could have even seen the soft glow as his ship glided through Nantasket Channel into the choppy dark blackness beyond.[29]

Good riddance.

CHAPTER 12

Skirmishes

*In which our hero partakes in patriotic
celebration before scoundrels strike a craven
blow, after which the Masons convene and a
murder unfolds on the cobbled streets of Boston.*

B ernard was gone. Half of the troops were gone. It
was finally time to celebrate.

The annual celebration of the Stamp Act resistance came
two weeks after the governor's departure. On Monday,
14 August 1769, Paul and the other Sons of Liberty converged around the Liberty Tree at eleven in the morning. Up
went the glasses and out went the toasts, one after another,
until fourteen were said. They upped the king and queen,
America and the Sons of Liberty, the Glorious Ninety-
two and the General Court. And they imprecated "the

Traducers of America" and "the late abandoned Fugitive," by whom they meant the governor. Once the toasts were completed, they crossed Boston Neck in a string of more than a hundred carriages and settled into an afternoon in Dorchester at Lemuel Robinson's Liberty Tree Tavern.[1]

On the field by the tavern, the Sons set up two rows of tables and stretched a sailcloth overhead. Colorful banners fluttered in the breezes and musicians sawed off tunes.[2]

Paul moved among the crowd, seeing one friend and then another. Several were customers, many fellow Masons. There was Joseph Warren. Cousin Thomas Hitchborn. Adam Colson. Josiah Flagg. There was Judge Richard Dana —who eight years before had fined Paul six shillings for roughing up Tom Fosdick. Joshua Brackett—who went Paul's bond back then—he was there too. And Samuel Adams and John Adams. Benjamin Edes and John Gill. Benjamin Church. James Otis. And still more patriot leaders, like Thomas Young and William Palfrey, John Hancock's clerk. There was John Hancock himself, decked out like a prince. Even John Singleton Copley—no radical, he—mixed among the throng. In all, the crowd numbered more than 350.[3]

There were plates to match. Three whole pigs were barbecued for the occasion, plus chickens and codfish. And cups of Madeira too. After dinner came the toasts— forty-five in all. Echoing those from the morning: first to the king, queen, and royal family—followed by a cannon shot and three cheers. Then: "North America and her fair Daughters of Liberty!" And: "John Wilkes, Esq." And:

"The Massachusetts Ninety-Two!" And: a whole string of defenders of liberty—local, in other colonies, and abroad—including resistance leaders in Corsica and Ireland.

They thrice cheered the merchants who foreswore imports and blasted cannon at mention of "the detested Names of the very few Importers," who should—went the toast—"be transmitted to posterity with Infamy."

Again they jabbed the governor, this time by name: "May Sir Francis Bernard of Nettleham, Baronet, the Commissioners and others his Confederates, the infamous Calumniators of North-America, soon meet with candign [proper] Punishment!" Up went three cheers.

"Success to the Manufactures of America"!

"The speedy Removal of all Task-Masters, and the Redress of all Grievances"!

"The Liberty of the PRESS"!

"The oppressed and distressed Protestants"!

"All true Patriots throughout the World"!

"The Abolition of all Craft and Low Cunning in Church or State"!

Finally: "Strong Halters, Firm Blocks, and Sharp Axes to all such as deserve either"! A cannon punctuated the last toast, and the men roared three cheers.[4]

Lucky that sailcloth. It began to rain. But for Revere and the others, there was no way to dampen the festivities. After the toasts, Nathaniel Balch offered entertainment, and Benjamin Church belted out the "Liberty Song," leading the whole throng in the chorus like some irregular choir.[5]

In freedom we're born and in freedom we'll live
Our purses are ready—steady, friends, steady
Not as slaves but as freemen our money we'll give.[6]

By late afternoon, they adjourned. Revere and the others clambered inside the waiting carriages and rolled for Boston. Hancock rode in a chariot at the lead; Otis rode in another at the rear.[7] They passed the guard house on Boston Neck and made for the Town House. The sun hung on till they arrived and trundled out. They assembled and marched around the seat of power like Joshua around Jericho. Then while the walls still stood, they melted into the streets, each for home.[8] Paul headed up to Clark's Wharf, probably with a clutch of fellow North Enders.

Bernard was, of course, not in the building. But he left poisonous traces of his rule. The day of the celebration, the *Boston Gazette* reported the arrival of a "new Freight of curious Letters of Sir Francis Bernard." More letters! But what was more curious were the other letters in the bundle. This new batch also contained correspondence from the customs officials, including one John Robinson.

Like Bernard's scribbles, John Robinson's painted the Sons of Liberty as traitors, Otis in particular. Otis had digested the accusations by Friday, 1 September, and demanded to speak with Robinson. He obliged. They met Saturday morning at the British Coffee House on King Street to sort things out. They left with things unsorted, though Robinson did suggest that he would give Otis satisfaction if he so desired. Satisfaction was the interest paid on insults. Otis commenced the collections process, but sloppily. Stewing on matters over the weekend, he called out Robinson in the pages of Monday's *Boston Gazette*. Now that he was also publicly insulted, it was Robinson's turn to demand satisfaction.[9]

The two met Tuesday night about seven at the British Coffee House. In the fistful of regulars, army and naval officers, customs agents, and other loyalists, Otis stuck out like a sore thumb.

When Robinson approached, Otis bolted to his feet, cane in hand. "I demand satisfaction of you, Sir," he boomed.

Robinson was fairly anxious to get his own.

After some back and forth, they decided to step out of the room to duke it out. But as they turned, Robinson reached up to tweak Otis's nose. Up went Otis's cane to push off Robinson's arm. Up went Robinson's cane to parry Otis's. Then they went at it. Cane cracked against cane in blow after blow until they took to bare knuckles. Lamps toppled in the scuffle. Tables too. Several of the other customers took Robinson's side and grabbed Otis, holding him back, drubbing him with fists, with canes, even with a sword—slicing a gash down to his skull. Otis staggered bloody under the blows.[10]

By the entrance walked a man named John Gridley, who saw the fracas unfolding. Shadowy masses lunged and pummeled at a man who looked like, like—James Otis!

"That's dirty usage!" he cried and shot inside to defend him.

In the thick someone grabbed Gridley, who reached out and snatched Robinson by the collar, ripping his coat. Down came the canes, the fists. He thrust up his arm to fend off a cane, and the blow broke his arm. The assailants then clutched him and chucked him headfirst out the door. But—hearing "Kill him! Kill him!"—the blood-streaked Gridley came back for more.[11]

By now a crowd was building and beginning to move toward the melee. Benjamin Hallowell, no friend of Otis, but uneager to see him murdered, somehow pulled him away from Robinson and helped him toward the door. Gridley, now back inside, pushed his way toward Otis, ready to give whatever he had left. With the intervention of Hallowell, Gridley, and now others, Robinson and attackers backdoored it and left the scene at a run.[12]

Boston was outraged by the attack.[13] Depositions were taken and arrests made, though Robinson somehow eluded sanction until he could leave for England.

Gashes and contusions sometimes replaced (and commonly augmented) arguments and imprecations in eighteenth-century Boston. Otis's treatment was far from unusual.

John Mein, publisher of the *Boston Chronicle*, obtained shipping manifests that showed boycotters importing forbidden goods. John Hancock was one of those singled out in the more than fifty manifests that Mein published. Hancock moved quickly to dispel any culpability and rally support for the boycott, but holding the line on non-importation while keeping the merchants in line was tough going. Preserving the effectiveness and viability of the boy-cotts meant ongoing maintenance of the nonimportation agreements, including Hancock's rearguard politicking to defend his actions.[14]

Keeping Mein in line was just as tough, and threats alone weren't cutting it. Fearing physical harm, Mein started carrying a pistol. It might have saved his life. While walking home from work with his business partner, he was accosted by William Molineaux and other patriots. A crowd massed. Mein pulled his pistol, and he and his partner retreated to the Main Guard, on King Street across from the Town House. They made it in the nick of time. Someone took a swing at Mein with a shovel blade, ven-tilated his coat and shirt, and sliced open his shoulder. Unable to do any worse to Mein, the patriots settled for tarring and feathering a suspected informer who unhappily was in the vicinity. Mein went into hiding and eventually sailed to England.[15]

Despite the efforts of loyalists like Mein, the nonimporta-tion efforts bore fruit. In 1769, imports were halved from the previous year.[16]

That was good for Revere. Fewer imports caused his services to be in greater demand. With tea on the outs, Paul made several silver coffeepots that year, including one

for Epes Sargent, two for Robert Hooper, and another for
Edward Cox and John Berry.[17] Revere crafted his coffeepots in the usual style, pear-shaped bodies, between ten
and thirteen inches tall, with elaborately sculpted spouts,
curved wooden handles, and adorned with the crest of the
purchaser, etched in a foliated frame.[18]

He also continued work for fellow Masons. In September,
the official papers recognizing the new Grand Lodge arrived
from Scotland. Revere was appointed the senior grand deacon, Joseph Warren the grand master. The lodge's jurisdic-
tion extended from Boston to "within one hundred miles of
the same." Eight other officers were chosen, for a total of
ten. All but two were also members of St. Andrew's, including Revere and Warren, so it's no surprise that St. Andrew's
helped the new lodge get its footing. Revere crafted the officers' jewels and the new lodge's seal. It took him some time
to get paid for the job, but no matter. The Masons were big
charity boosters—having, for instance, in summer and fall
that year, given one widow more than £11—but they would
pay Paul soon enough.[19] He was pretty intent on getting
paid, especially when he had a purchase in mind.

The installations came at year's end, on 27 December,
the feast day for St. John the Evangelist.[20] Masons assembled at the Green Dragon. There were Paul, Thomas
Crafts, and other friends. And in one of those quirks of
occupation, two British officers were also there to be in-
stalled as officers. They were part of the group Revere and
Warren had met with the previous November. Warren gave
a grand speech, and festivities followed.[21]

It was a great way to end the year. And Paul had just the trick to start the new one off. Fewer imports plus the influx of troops and their money meant that Paul pulled in enough cash in 1769 to finally buy a house—though not enough to avoid a sizable mortgage. Paul borrowed £160 of the £214 price. It was in the same neighborhood as his shop, on North Square just a block back from Clark's Wharf, where he continued to rent his shop. The house was old, built the previous century, but it was sturdy and spacious enough for Paul's ever-growing family.[22]

At the time of the purchase, Deborah was almost twelve and would have been a godsend around the house, helping to keep eyes on the other children. Her little brother, Paul, was just ten and old enough to help dad around the shop between hours at school—just like his father had at that age. Little Sarah had just celebrated her eighth birthday, and Frances's fourth was only days away. Toddler Mary's was the following month.[23]

Aside from making room for his growing family, buying a home also helped Paul's social ascent. Several of Boston's upper crust lived in the vicinity. The father of Harvard's president lived on the street. The Cockerel sat directly behind Paul's house, and Pastor Pemberton, whose shepherding Paul now avoided, lived across the square. Thomas Hutchinson himself lived right around the corner. Also true to form in the North End, many of Paul's new neighbors were just as common as he—a couple of tailors, a bricklayer, some merchants, mast makers, and spinsters. Another goldsmith lived in the neighborhood, Benjamin

Burt. He was a patriot like Paul and a member, also like Paul, of the North End Caucus.[24]

Guaranteed, Paul and Burt and the rest of the North End Caucus heard heated discussions at the start of the new year about nonimportation. The existing boycott was scheduled to run only through 1769. Come 1770, merchants had to re-up. And they didn't want to.

Merchants lost money because of the policy, and many refused to back the boycotts, or they said one thing and did another. Violating the nonimportation agreements was a constant problem and undermined the patriot cause—especially when hypocrisy was outed.

Some merchants were open about their refusal to back the boycotts. As the town polarized around its politics, this could be a problem. In one case a group of boys and young men started harassing a loyalist merchant for his refusal to join the boycott. They pelted his store with rocks and picketed with signs.

Who should come along but his neighbor, the customs snitch Ebenezer Richardson? He tried dispersing the crowd, but then had rocks headed his direction. He ducked and ran a few doors down to his home and took refuge inside. The boys followed and started chucking eggs and knocking out his windows with rocks. One stone hit his wife. Richardson took his gun—loaded with heavy birdshot—and yelled from the second-story window: "By God I'll make a Lane through you."[25]

And then he did.

The gun belched its missiles. A boy fell, as blood escaped the pea-sized punctures in his chest and ran through the torn fibers of his shirt onto the cold cobbled street.[26]

CHAPTER 13

Massacre

*In which the oil-and-water mixture of soldier
and civilian turns turbulent and spills into bloody
confrontations at which time our hero engraves
a shocking scene of horror and shame.*

The *Boston Gazette* reported that the funeral for young Christopher Seider would start from his parents' house "opposite Liberty Tree," so that "all the friends of Liberty may have an opportunity of paying their last Respects to the Remains of this little Hero and first martyr to the noble Cause. . . ."[1] The word *martyr* comes from the Greek word for witness. The title fits a first-century Christian chucked to the lions rather than renounce his faith. It's a bit of a stretch to a rabble-rousing kid chucking rocks, but patriot leaders like Sam Adams pulled for all they could get. They patterned the event after the funeral for the St. George's Field victims. Between four and five hundred children marched in procession as the coffin was carried to its final resting place, every one of their long, pale faces an accusation and a curse.[2]

The funeral at the tail end of February may have laid Seider to rest, but the rest of the town remained agitated. Two days into March, on Friday, a soldier named Patrick Walker strolled past the Gray's Ropewalks manufactory. One of the rope makers, William Green, asked if he wanted work.

"Yes," he said. "I do, faith."

"Well," sassed Green, "then go and clean my s—t house."

"Empty it yourself," snarled Walker.

And then they ran to it, fists flying. But Walker was outnumbered by the other rope makers, beaten, disarmed, and sent running away, swearing "by the Holy Ghost" that he'd be back for revenge.[3]

It wasn't long, and Walker returned with eight or nine redcoats in tow, including one Private Matthew Kilroy. But Green had backup, too, among them Samuel Gray. And the soldiers and the rope makers traded blows, the redcoats wielding their cutlasses and clubs, the rope makers their stout wouldering sticks, used in making cable.

The rope makers bested the soldiers. The redcoats retreated, regrouped, and came back with still more men.

Rope makers from nearby manufactories came to the aid of their fellows, and the soldiers suffered yet another rout. So it went throughout the day. Sporadic fights spilled into Saturday, finally cooling on Sunday. But nothing was settled.[4] On Monday, 5 March, the soldiers distributed a handbill informing

> ye Rebellious People in Boston that ye Soldjers . . . are determined to Joine together and defend themselves against all who shall Oppose them.[5]

Before the day was out, they'd get their chance.

Monday was a cold day. About a foot of snow had settled, thawed through the afternoon, and then frozen again into the evening, leaving a thick crust of ice on the streets. The chill didn't prevent many from running their errands and going about their business even well past nightfall. But people were visibly nervy, as if they expected something to happen.

A bit of a moon was up. A lone sentry, Private Hugh White, waited by his guardbox outside the Custom House. The customs officials worked from the Concert Hall but held their collections at the Custom House, just one block down King Street from the Town House.

A little after eight o'clock, a young man came by and made a stink about one of the officers not paying his bills. The kid thought the officer was inside and was there to collect if he could. White took up the officer's defense. Words went back and forth. Finally White smacked the kid upside his head with the stock of his musket, and the boy took off bawling.

On Brattle Street, not far from where White stood, a clutch of soldiers and stick-wielding citizens renewed the earlier brawls. They traded cracking, thudding blows. As the situation boiled over, someone hoisted a boy through a window at the Old Brick Meetinghouse. He started cranking away on the bell. All the gonging and clanging normally meant a fire had caught and was spreading. Out their doors poured men with their leather buckets ready to help extinguish the blaze. But where? Where was the fire? They spilled into King Street, by the Town House, looking for direction. But there was no fire. It was "only a rumpus with the soldiers," someone said. False alarm.

"Every man to his home!" came the cry.[6]

But others were pouring into King Street with cudgels and sticks. The boy, his ear still smarting from White's blow, was with them.

"Here is the soldier who did it!" said one.

The boy pointed at White. "This is the soldier who knocked me down with the butt-end of his musket," he said.

"Kill him! Knock him down!"[7]

People began gathering, massing, shouting. They pinned White on the Custom House steps against the door and left him ducking snowballs and dodging chunks of ice. A tall man described variously as an Indian or mulatto was there,

View of King Street, the scene of the Boston Massacre.
Library of Congress.

Crispus Attucks. He was carrying a long stick with which he started jabbing White, calling him "lobster," and saying he'd "have one of his claws off."[8]

White loaded his firelock.

"The lobster is going to fire," said a boy in the crowd.

Henry Knox, a local bookseller, walked onto the scene and tried to calm matters, but no one seemed to listen. Everything was ready to explode.

Captain Thomas Preston enjoyed an evening at the Concert Hall. After retiring to his lodgings, he got wind that people were harassing one of his sentries in the street by the Custom House. He strapped on his sword and made for the Main Guard, just up the street from the mob, which, as he could see when he arrived, swelled by the second. There were about fifty to sixty massed against White. Preston gathered a group of grenadier privates and one corporal— seven men in total, eight counting himself—and marched up to rescue White.[9] Private Matthew Kilroy was in the bunch.

Knox saw the men marching and ran to meet them. He came up to Preston and grabbed him by the coat. Preston stopped.

"For God's sake take care of your men," said Knox. "If they fire, you die."

"I am sensible of it," Preston snapped. He turned to catch up with his men.[10]

The troop pushed through the crushing crowd—"Make way"—their bayonets out—"d—n you"—one brushing the hat of Paul's friend and colleague Nathaniel Hurd— "make way. . . ." They shoved their way past another of Paul's friends, Nate Fosdick. Finally in front of the Custom House, the redcoats congealed in a clot around the besieged private and faced the taunters.[11]

It was just like the scene at St. George's Field, except the mob here more frenzied, the air more charged. The people pressed in till the bayonet tips pricked their chests. Many held clubs and wouldering sticks and beat them together in threatening thwacks and cracks.[12]

"Come on, you Rascals, you bloody-backs," they cried.

"Fire if you dare, G—d d—n you."

"D—n you, you sons of b—s, fire."

"You can't kill us all."[13]

Preston tried shouting, but his words couldn't cut through the thicket of curses and taunts or those wretched bells that kept banging away. He could hardly raise his voice enough to be heard, let alone reason with the mob. He needed to get an advantage, fast.

People threw snowballs, ice, even clubs and sticks. One of the clubs hit a grenadier so hard it knocked him down. He dropped his weapon. Up he jumped, spitting mad, clutched his musket and yelled, "D—n you, fire!"—and pulled the trigger.

The flintlock flash was like a shot of lightning, and the mob got sucked into that frantic stillness and dread antici-pation that follows. Other than little scuffles on the line, shuffling feet, surging one way, then the next, eyes dart-ing every which way, looking for direction, cues, anything, everything held for a moment. Just a moment. Then: the bone-jarring rumble of thunder.

Private Matthew Kilroy was in the line. He laid an eye on one of his foes from the previous days' rumbles, Sam Gray. Up went his musket. He drew a bead and pulled the trigger. Out the barrel blew a leaden ball that flew faster than sound and plunged into Gray's skull. The force shat-tered the bone, cracked his head wide open, and spun him on his heels. His legs gave way, and he fell to the snow. Then the other redcoats let it rip. Scattered, staccato gun-fire sent lead balls whizzing into the dense mass of flesh and bone before them. There were screams, cries, and the muted sound of bodies hitting ground. Blood soaked the snow like wine on a table linen.[14]

Through the ghostly haze of the dissipating gunsmoke and by the sickly light of the slivered moon, people saw shapes against the snow, some writhing, some not—Sam Gray, Crispus Attucks, Samuel Maverick, James Caldwell, Patrick Carr, Edward Payne, Christopher Monk, John Green, David Parker, others. Gray and Attucks were already dead. So were Caldwell and Maverick. Carr took a ball to his hip; he hung on. Payne took a shot to the arm that shattered the bone. Parker took a ball to the thigh.

It was bedlam. People scampered away from the line of fire, halving like the Red Sea. The bells started again, and people spilled out of doors and into the streets. Then the sea closed, and men rushed back in to gather up the dead and the dying, while soldiers re-formed their line and scrambled to their barracks on Preston's orders.[15]

A few people bolted north the half mile to Revere's neighborhood, to Hutchinson's house, and pleaded with him—"for God's sake"—to intervene. There may be an out-and-out war between citizens and soldiers if you don't get down there now! Just as when he risked life and limb over the Stamp Act riot at Oliver's house, Hutchinson steeled himself as best he could and took off for King Street.

Back outside the Main Guard, Preston ordered a new batch of soldiers to ready for an assault. They filed up in a street-fighting formation in front of the Main Guard down to the corner of the Town House.

Hutchinson meanwhile strode through the crowd and listened to what voices he could understand, seeing all that his eyes could capture. There were four dead; another several were badly wounded. But the scene was too noisy, too crazed. Hutchinson made for the Town House and the council chamber. From there he walked to the side of the building to the balcony overlooking the scene of the carnage. The soldiers were down to his right, where they stood in formation. The people to his left. Justice would be done, he told them. Indeed, Preston and the soldiers were shortly arrested and bound over for trial. But wounds so fresh and inflicted by those so loathed would never be salved by mere words.

In the days that followed, ink rushed in a thousand tributaries. Adams, Otis, Warren were familiar fonts, penning torrents in private letters and in public venues like the *Boston Gazette.*

Revere played his part. He went to work immediately. Edes and Gill asked him to engrave pictures of coffins for the dead: Sam Gray, Samuel Maverick, James Caldwell, and Crispus Attucks. Paul marked them with their initials, each with a skull and crossbones underneath.[16]

About the same time, for the use in the investigation and trials, Paul drew a scene of the killings. He detailed how the troops were arrayed, standing in a semicircle, their guns pointing outward. He showed where four of the five bodies fell of the men who died. Two directly in front of the troops. Another three-quarters across the street. Another fully across King Street, in Quaker Lane, between shops that fronted King Street.[17] Then Patrick Carr died, and Paul etched another coffin for the *Gazette.*[18]

It wasn't Paul's only work to come from the shooting.

The Boston painter and engraver, Henry Pelham, illustrated a detailed picture of the massacre. It's a large and emotionally striking picture that shows redcoats arrayed against the people, their guns leveled in a professional manner, the words "Custom House" behind them, over their shoulders, establishing the scene. Great blasts of gun smoke cloud the scene, the weapons discharged and the order of a commander raising his sword. The people are fallen back, some down on the ground with wounds issuing blood; some helping others; some simply dead. It wasn't actually

Paul Revere's engraving of the Boston Massacre.
Library of Congress.

how the men fell, nor how the soldiers stood; Revere's diagram of the scene makes that clear. But it communicated what the people of Boston felt—that the event was a deliberate act of murder.

When Pelham finished after several days of work, he left his creation with Paul Revere. The reasons why are unclear. What happened next, however, is clear enough. Paul did what he usually did—what most engravers did—he started copying. Revere etched a copy of the Pelham design and, without consulting him, began selling it. His figures aren't as graceful. His faces, less lifelike. But the emotional power of Revere's work was potentially even greater. Paul, for instance, over the "Custom House" added more signage: "Butcher's Hall." Pelham was outraged and fired off a stinging letter to Revere. Whatever bad blood came of the copying, however, seems to have not lasted long, and the two reached a settlement for any damages. To this day, Revere's version—titled *The Bloody Massacre*—is the better known.[19]

A month following the killing on King Street, Revere also engraved a scene of the troops landing in 1768, an elaborate image that shows an ocean view of Boston, two-thirds of it, all of the North End on the right, moving across the page with part of the South End to the left. It shows eight ships arrayed in the harbor, with their guns facing the town and streams of boats bringing redcoats to shore, muskets and bayonets up, pricking the sky.

Given the recent bloodshed, Revere's dedication to the secretary of state for America seems more a jab than gift:

To the Earl of Hillsborough, His Majests. Secy. Of State for America. This View of the only well Plan'd Expedition, formed for supporting ye dignity of Britain & chastising ye insolence of America, is hum'y Inscrib'd.[20]

This image taken with *The Bloody Massacre* engraving left no doubt. London was in the wrong for sending the troops, and the evidence was first frozen red in the snow of King Street but now in the ink of Paul's prints.

The court saw it differently. The trials were slow in coming, but they finally arrived. Convinced the men required a fair trial, John Adams represented the troops admirably. Preston was acquitted in October 1770. The patriots groaned.

Maybe song lightened the heavy mood. Revere again engraved plates for a music book. This one, for William Billings, was the most elaborate yet. *The New-England Psalm-Singer* included 116 pages, and Revere engraved all the words and music. While he left no record of it, the length of the project probably meant he was well paid for his work. Back in 1765 he charged Josiah Flagg £150 for just half the engraving of 66 pages.

For Billings, Paul created an image—unlike most of his illustrations—of his own design. It's simplistic and shows seven men sitting around a table, holding four sheets of music between them and singing. Around that image is a staff of music in an oval with these words:

Wake every Breath & every String.
To bless the great Redeemer King.
His Name thro' every Clime ador'd:
Let Joy & Gratitude, and Love,
Thro' all the Notes of Music rove:
And JESUS sound on every Chord.

The book contained other hymns, anthems, and psalms, including Psalm 23. The way things were shaking out, Revere and the patriots probably felt the need for a shepherd and still waters; every cue indicated that they were walking through the valley of the shadow.[21] The nonimportation agreement, for one example, disintegrated in the fall. And for another, the remainder of the troops were either acquitted or convicted on lesser charges by December. How to make matters worse? Hutchinson was formally made governor of the province in December. It was going to be a dreary winter.

Perhaps the only bright moment that same dark month: little Elizabeth joined the Revere family. She was baptized 9 December at West Church.

CHAPTER 14

Ebb

In which the fortunes of the patriots turn and a
tempest starts stirring in its proverbial pot
while tragedy coils like a snake before
striking the heart of our forlorn hero.

The Boston Massacre and the events leading up to it became the central event of the patriot experience. The date of 5 March replaced 14 August's Stamp Act resistance, even 18 March's repeal of the Stamp Act. It became the Good Friday of the patriots' liturgical year. All of the various offenses and outrages had been cousined together under this day.[1] But they lived in perpetual Saturday. There was no resurrection yet; their hopes lay in the grave.

To mark the day in 1771, Thomas Young gave a stirring oration, and Revere exhibited several transparencies or "illuminations." On the evening of the anniversary he placed them in the lead casement windows of his North Square home. With a lantern behind them, they glowed to passersby a haunting series of scenes: one the ghost of young Seider, his finger jabbed in his own wound, trying to stanch the flow of blood, his friends weeping nearby. The next window showed the massacre itself, a scene similar to his engraving, blood streaming from the wounds of the fallen. The final window showed a woman representing America. She sat upon a tree stump and held a staff with a liberty cap, similar to the image for Edes and Gill's almanac. A redcoat lies at her feet, one of hers upon his head, and in his hand a serpent.

From the evening display until Paul closed the show at ten o'clock upon the ringing of church bells, "many Thousands," according to the *Boston Gazette*, came by to view. They were "struck with Solem Silence & their Countenances covered with a meloncholy Gloom." And then everyone went home.[2]

In more ways than one.

Despite outward shows like the massacre anniversary, after the boycott petered out, so did the patriots. People lost the nerve, lost the patience, lost the interest.

Revere's business increased in 1771. It was the usual mix of buckles, buttons, cups, tankards, teapots, and assorted silverware. Only more so. He continued to work with people of any politics, and loyalists helped build up his business in the years following the massacre. Not that his politics changed. He continued his participation with the Sons of Liberty even when others did not or befell hardship. Sam Adams, for instance, hit a rough patch. He faced a turncoat loyalist in a local election and lost badly.[3] James Otis's health, particularly his mental health, failed him.[4] Hancock's patriotic ardor cooled, and he drifted for a time into Hutchinson's camp.[5] At least one other prominent Son of Liberty did as well, but no one then knew.

But while the patriot cause stalled and faltered, there is nothing so relentless as politics. Despite the lull, Paul's involvement with the North End Caucus continued to grow. Votes throughout 1772 reveal a good deal of politicking. The caucus would meet and galvanize opinion of the members around a political candidate or a policy and thereby influence the official town meeting or General Court. From the earliest records, Paul was voted onto committees and vested with responsibilities for the group, including communications with the South End Caucus.[6]

From the members' roll, it's clear that several of his caucus mates were fellow Masons, such as Thomas Young, Joseph Warren, and Benjamin Edes. Paul's life in those circles continued to confer upon him added responsibilities as well. During 1771 he served as master of St. Andrew's and at the end of the year, 6 December, the Massachusetts Grand Lodge elected him one of two grand deacons for the year of 1772.[7]

On 24 June 1772, Revere and Warren and the rest of the Massachusetts Grand Lodge celebrated the feast day of John the Baptist. They started by gathering with fellow lodge members at the Concert Hall, decked in their Masonic regalia, and processed up to North Church, where Paul rang bells when he was a boy of fifteen. Once settled in the pews, the men listened to visiting minister Rev. Samuel Fayerweather preach "a very suitable and pertinent discourse" before they adjourned to the Green Dragon. Like the festivities at Robinson's Liberty Tree Tavern, the Masons stretched a cloth overhead in the spacious garden out back, which extended all the way to Mill Pond. "[T]he remainder of the day was dedicated to Mirth and Social Festivity."[8]

But it wasn't mere partying. Through organizations like the caucus and the Masons, the patriots forged the community spirit necessary for their movement to propel itself forward, particularly in tough times. Those bonds would have to be strong for what was coming.

For much of 1772 there had been reports and speculation that governors would be receiving salaries from the Crown—thus freeing them from any accountability to the local assemblies, like the General Court. In the last decade the patriots had done a solid job of infecting these bodies. So much so that an irritated Thomas Hutchinson referred to them as "Lilliputian" assemblies—many, small, and pestiferous. The patriots couldn't count on any help or reconsideration from London. They'd been petitioning London for years now about various overreaches or injustices and were finally getting the message: drop dead.[9]

What to do? A town meeting would be held 28 October 1772. Otis and John Adams met the day before at the offices of the *Boston Gazette*. Revere was at this meeting before the meeting, though he was not allowed inside for the secret proceedings. He and Edes and Gill watched the door while the patriot leaders schemed about a response to royal salaries.[10]

The colonies would have to turn to each other. When Boston again gathered at the town meeting 2 November 1772, Sam Adams moved for the creation of a Committee of Correspondence—an official body that would link the disparate colonies through communication, informing each and all about local repressions and overreaches by the government.[11] The town meeting appointed the committee members for Boston that same day. In short order, similar bodies sprang up all over New England. And not just there.

Adams's need for such a committee was affirmed by merchants in Rhode Island. They had recently torched the *Gaspée*, an armed schooner that the Crown had sent to put a stop to smuggling in those waters.[12] Britain responded by appointing a Commission of Inquiry—essentially a grand jury—to investigate, level charges, and ship the subjects off to England for prosecution. But no one talked, and the commission failed. It did serve one use: Virginia took note and also urged the founding of a Committee of Correspondence. Too much was bubbling in all of the colonies. The patriots had to keep track of it and form a common understanding of what was occurring to them, lest they be put at a disadvantage by their ignorance.[13] Soon all the colonies were linked in a web of intelligence collecting and dispersal.

In November Paul took in a dance at Newburyport to celebrate a friend's wedding.[14] Sarah apparently stayed home, as she was late in her eighth pregnancy. Little Isanna came shortly after, on 15 December 1772. Unlike most of the children, she wasn't baptized for several weeks—not until 17 January. Perhaps her health wasn't the best. Sarah had a hard go of the delivery and declined in the weeks that followed the birth.

It was a portent of troubles to come.

For starters, Revere found himself embroiled in a fractious and unhappy matter: a dispute with one William Burbeck over the Green Dragon and the possession of St. Andrew's Masonic charter.[15]

While that controversy boiled, so did another, with far-reaching consequences. The Townshend Acts had been repealed in 1770. But the tea provisions stood. Now on 29 March 1773, the *Boston Gazette* reported about a bill called the Tea Act, essentially a massive financial rescue mission for the British East India Company, a private corporation of merchants whose efforts had colonized India for the Crown, similar to John Winthrop's in Massachusetts.[16]

Throughout the late 1760s, inefficiency, incompetence, and corruption crippled the company. By the fall of 1772, it owed the government more than £1 million. London pushed a bailout package that extended a massive loan—well over what was already owed—and more control over the company's governance. It also allowed the East India Company the freedom to sell tea directly to the Americas rather than to auction houses in England.

Four American cities were set to receive the tea: Charleston, Philadelphia, New York, and Boston. It was sold on consignment to groups of merchants in each locale. For Boston the consignees included Thomas and Elisha Hutchinson—sons of the governor. Hutchinson had, in fact, used his pull to get them the gig.[17]

But there was still that nettlesome issue of the tax on tea to deal with. Parliament decided to keep that in place, much to the chagrin of the patriots in the several colonies.

While these private and public battles raged, personal losses loomed. In mid-spring 1773, Joseph Warren's wife, Elizabeth, died. On 3 May, within days of her passing, the *Boston Gazette* announced her burial and carried a tribute poem by the widower Warren:

> These virtues fallen enhance the scene of woe,
> Swell the big drops that scarce confinement know,
> And force them down in copious showers to flow.[18]

Revere consoled his friend, but then found blackened occasion to share in his grief. Only a week after Elizabeth shed the mortal coil, hours after the ink of Warren's tribute dried on the pages of the *Gazette*, Paul's own Sarah—wife of sixteen years, mother of their eight children—also died. She was thirty-seven years old.[19]

CHAPTER 15

Flow

*In which our disheartened hero patches together
his life, courts a fetching new love, while
the events of fate tax the patriots anew,
test their resolve, and force
a destructive hand in Boston Harbor.*

Revere wasn't getting on well.

Professionally he was fine. Within a week of burying his dear Sarah, he stood at his workbench, engraving hat bills and making silver hooks and eyes.[1] Money needed earning, and memories needed distraction. If diversion helped, Paul helped himself.

He was also okay socially. He jumped into civic and political life with both boots. The Grand Lodge gave him a boost when it ruled against William Burbeck in their dispute and suspended him.[2] On 18 May Revere joined a committee involved with erecting street lamps through-out Boston. He was chosen with several others to identify the best locations in the North End.[3] Just days after that, Revere hung out with caucus mates William Molineaux and William Dennie. The trio razzed Benjamin Hallowell and another customs commissioner as they left dinner at Concert Hall. What's life without harassing the customs man?[4] Around this time he also put up a barn in his back-yard and bought a horse.[5]

The trouble was more domestic. He struggled with life as a single father. Despite the help of both Deborahs, mother and eldest daughter, there was too much to manage. Isanna wasn't thriving. The other children needed attention. The house was, as two of his grandsons later recalled, "in sore need of a mother's care. . . ."[6]

And then he found her, and it wasn't one of the spin-sters on his block.

He might have known her for years, as her family lived in the area, but as the story goes, he rushed home from work one evening and ran into her at North Square. She was beautiful, with a high forehead, narrow chin, and dainty smile. The attraction was immediate. Paul suggested that she follow him back home. He seemed anxious to get moving, said he wanted to be with his children before they went to bed. That must have been endearing. She followed. Of course he was charming, with his brown eyes and dark complexion. But it was the family that she found too sweet and needy to resist. Little Isanna, so delicate and frail. The children with only grandmother and big sis to see to their needs. She stayed for the evening. She stayed for many others as well.[7]

Paul was smitten. He whiled away, letting his mind turn over the possibilities, all the little pictures and plans of the future. Working in his shop and seized by one of those moments, he grabbed an old bill, dipped his quill, and started scribbling the most unlikely love poem on the reverse:

> Take three fourths of a Paine that makes Traitors
>   confess
> With three parts of a place which the Wicked don't
>   Bless
> Joyne four sevenths of an Exercise which shop-
>   keepers use
> Add what Bad Men do, when they good Actions
>   refuse
> These four added together with great care and Art
> Will point out the Fair One that is nearest my Heart.[8]

Here's the great care and art: the first is *rack*, three-fourths of which is *rac*; the second is *hell*, three parts of which is *hel*; the third is *walking*, four-sevenths of which is *walk*; and what do bad men do when they refuse good actions? Why, naturally, they *err*. Drop the second *r* and you can see what he's getting at: *Rac–hel–Walk–er*.

Eleven years his junior, almost to the day, Rachel Walker came from a good family and seemed intent to make Paul a good wife. Their meeting at the North Square couldn't have come a moment too soon. Paul was in desperate need.

The patriot cause languished, but London kept giving them reason to galvanize. While Paul was courting Rachel, the Bernard letters scandal recapitulated like a theme in tragic opera. This time letters from the pens of Thomas Hutchinson and a handful of officials found their way back to Boston. They were first aired in a secret session of the General Court. But by mid-June, Revere and the rest of Boston could purchase a copy of thirteen of the letters, bound as a pamphlet with the improbably long title:

COPY OF LETTERS SENT TO GREAT-BRITAIN, BY HIS EXCELLENCY THOMAS HUTCHINSON, THE HON. ANDREW OLIVER, AND SEVERAL OTHER PERSONS, BORN AND EDUCATED AMONG US IN WHICH (NOTWITHSTANDING HIS EXCELLENCY'S DECLARATION TO THE HOUSE, THAT THE TENDENCY AND DESIGN OF THEM WAS NOT TO SUBVERT THE CONSTITUTION, BUT RATHER TO PRESERVE IT ENTIRE) THE JUDICIOUS READER WILL DISCOVER THE FATAL SOURCE OF THE CONFUSION AND BLOODSHED IN WHICH THIS PROVINCE ESPECIALLY HAS BEEN INVOLVED, AND WHICH THREATENED TOTAL DESTRUCTION TO THE LIBERTIES OF ALL AMERICA.

The promised revelation about the Boston Massacre failed to materialize, but the "judicious reader" could find troubling stuff nonetheless.

In the letters, Hutchinson disparaged "the licentiousness of such as call themselves Sons of Liberty." He spoke of the necessity of abridging "what is called English liberty." And he argued that either "Parliament must give up its claim to a supreme authority over the colonies or the colonies must cease from asserting a supreme legislative within themselves."[9] No prizes for guessing which course he preferred, or for guessing the reaction from the patriots. They started by burning Hutchinson in effigy and even had him impeached, petitioning the Crown to remove him from office.[10]

Take the salary fight, the letters, and then add tea. In late June came news that the Tea Act bailout package had passed Parliament.[11] The scalding mixture was ready to spill through Boston's lanes—but not before another tragedy and another blessing.

Little Isanna, the child who'd struggled since her birth in December, passed away on 19 September 1773. In the thick of grief, Paul turned ever more to Rachel. They married less than a month later, on 10 October 1773. And Revere renewed the distance from the Cockerel's loyalist minister Pemberton, instead being wed by the radical Rev. Simeon Howard at Mayhew's old West Church pulpit.

Back in England, merchants lined up ships to transport the tea to the colonies. James Scott, one of Hancock's captains, refused his ship. But plenty of others offered theirs.[12] By mid-October, the *Dartmouth*, the *Eleanor*, and the *Beaver* cut the Atlantic waves with several hundred crates of tea in their holds.[13]

In Boston, hackles raised about the tea, and plans for

resistance hatched up and down town. The North End Caucus met 23 October, and Revere, Warren, and the others voted to "oppose the vending any Tea, sent by the East India Company to any part of the Continent, with our lives and fortunes."[14]

They reaffirmed their vote Tuesday, 2 November, and met to discuss strategy. Earlier that day, in the wee hours, messengers had pounded upon the doors of the consignees (those commissioned to sell the tea) and informed them that the town expected their presence at the foot of the Liberty Tree on Wednesday to resign their commissions. The event was announced all over town. The following day the North End Caucus voted to "get a flag of Liberty Tree." Theirs wasn't the only one. Some five hundred people, including Adams, Hancock, Warren, and the town selectmen, showed up Wednesday to watch the event, and the tree was streaming with banners. To no effect. The consignees failed to show.

In the following days, the patriots politicked it the best they could, going back and forth with the consignees. The North End Caucus, the town meeting, and other clubs pushed the ship's owner and the local merchants responsible for the shipments for a positive resolution—namely, preventing the tea from landing and the duties paid.

It wasn't proving effectual. But they had no alternatives. The colonists would have to do for themselves. Petitioning for redress was now thought "degrading." The Crown never paid attention. Parliament was set against them. The *Massachusetts Spy* asked if colonists should "whine and cry for relief, when we have already tried in vain?"[15] The answer was no.

Then the first tea ship arrived. The *Dartmouth*. It was 28 November. No way the patriots were going to allow the tea to be offloaded. The town meeting affirmed their resistance with formal resolutions, insisting that the tea "should not be landed; that it should be sent back in the same bottom to the place whence it came, at all events, and that no duty should be paid on it."[16]

To make sure the tea stayed aboard, the North End Caucus established a rotating guard of just over two dozen men to patrol and prevent the tea from being offloaded. Revere was one of the guards.[17] The ship's owner, Francis Rotch, had every reason to get the tea off his boat. The law mandated that the duty be paid within twenty days of landing. That meant he had through 16 December. Otherwise the customs men could seize his cargo.

The clock was ticking, and all parties involved jockeyed for an advantage. The patriots wanted the ship to simply set sail for England. But the customs men wouldn't let that happen without the tea offloaded and the taxes paid. It was the law. Hutchinson wouldn't let the *Dartmouth* turn around either, or the *Eleanor* or the *Beaver* when they arrived, each bearing even more tea. The patriots and the importers were at an impasse.

Clouds massed in the skies over Boston the morning of 14 December. It was a Tuesday. Handbills across town called "Friends! Brethren! Countrymen!" to an afternoon confab at the Old South Meetinghouse.

The church bells rang at 2:00 p.m., and a sea of citizens washed inside. Patriot leaders grilled the captain of the *Eleanor* and *Dartmouth* owner Francis Rotch about getting clearances from the customs men for their ships to leave the harbor without offloading the tea or paying the duties. They both indicated they would try to get the passes for their ships. But by day's end, it appeared it would take more time, and time needed no clearance. It was already fleeing like the outbound tide. The *Dartmouth*'s deadline was just two days away, midnight, 16 December.[18]

The patriots adjourned till Thursday morning, the sixteenth. At 10:00 a.m., more than three thousand locals pushed inside the meetinghouse; another two thousand came in from the neighboring countryside towns. The clouds fell, and rain streaked the windows of the building.[19]

Rotch was there with news that no clearance was forthcoming from the customs men. The patriots told him to go straight to Governor Hutchinson, who was then in Milton at his country home. Out walked Rotch into the downpour. He made the journey to Milton in the cold wet—a three-hour ride in good weather—to a reception about as welcoming. Hutchinson and Rotch tried to work it out but could not reach agreement.

Early Thursday evening, a few Masons converged on the Green Dragon. Those who arrived for the usual Masonic meeting found so few of their fellows there that they adjourned early. It's not that the other Masons weren't there. It's just that they were downstairs in another room with members of the North End Caucus, planning. Anticipating Rotch's arrival, they soon broke up and made their way back to Old South Meetinghouse. They weren't expecting good news.[20]

As twilight descended upon the town, so did Rotch. He crossed Boston Neck, filed up the main road, and worked his way toward Old South Meetinghouse. The Green Dragon schemers were right. Once inside, Rotch informed the town meeting that Hutchinson denied the pass.[21]

Up stood Sam Adams.

"This meeting," he said, every ear in the place taking in the sound, "can do nothing more to save the country."[22]

It was a cue. Out in the street came a bloodcurdling cry like an Indian war whoop. Then the call: "Boston Harbor a teapot tonight!"

And: "The Mohawks are come!"

And: "Hurrah for Griffin's Wharf!"

And down the streets they swarmed toward Griffin's Wharf, dozens and dozens of red-ochre'd and lampblacked men disguised as Indians, Revere in the forefront, with hundreds of townsfolk in their train, including Paul's own thirteen-year-old son and namesake, Paul Jr.[23]

Revere and the Mohawks boarded the *Dartmouth*, the *Eleanor*, and the *Beaver*. Each ship had more than a hun-

The Boston Tea Party.
Library of Congress.

dred crates of tea in her hold, more than ninety thousand pounds of the stuff. The Indians went straight to work. They opened the hatches and hoisted the crates to the decks. Men with hatchets—*crack!*—busted them—*crack!*—open and tipped the boxes overboard, one after another after another after another. They were at it for two solid hours, but by the time they were done, nearly every ounce was brewing in the briny bay.

The men were careful not to destroy any other property and restored what little damage they did. The entire episode was orderly—almost a perfect counterpoint to the riots of previous years. No doubt this owed to the careful orchestration and oversight of men like Adams and Warren and the execution of a handful of lieutenants like Revere.

The job now was to alert sister colonies. In the hours that followed, Sam Adams sat down and started scribbling the news for the Committee of Correspondence, so fast he sometimes literally failed to dot i's and cross t's or even punctuate.

"We conceived it our duty to afford you the most early advice of this interesting event by express," penned Adams to patriot leaders in New York and Philadelphia.[24] The news was to be carried by express.

As to the express rider himself, "The bearer is chosen by the committee from a number of gentlemen, who volunteered to carry you this intelligence."[25]

That gentleman was Revere.

And over Boston Neck he flew.

CHAPTER 16

Express

*In which our hero, thrust into a new role,
becomes known far and wide—
even in lands across the stormy sea—as the
messenger of the Revolution, while the
Crown cracks down with merciless resolve.*

Winter weather scowled at travelers. Revere scowled right back. To be effective, express riders had to be swift. This was Paul's first time out. He tore up the road. Bundled against the rain and the chill winds, he never slowed as he made the two-hundred-mile trek past leafless birches and naked elms to New York.

He delivered Adam's epistle to his New York compatriots. It contained all the key elements but was short on detail. Always up for a story, Paul no doubt filled in the gaps.

He stayed several days at the home of fellow Son of Liberty John Lamb, and by the end of his sojourn he'd converted his host to fast friend. They had more than their politics in common. Lamb was a wine merchant, but like Revere, he also engraved copperplate. Revere's telling of the Tea Party was evidently so compelling that Lamb etched a plate of the party from the account.[1]

Revere returned on 27 December, the feast day of St. John the Evangelist. Paul had an *evangel* of his own. Lamb wasn't the only one sympathetic to Boston's position; all the New York patriots backed Boston. No tea would land there or in Philadelphia.[2]

Boston welcomed Paul's report. The morning of the twenty-eighth, every church bell in town sent its big round peals rolling through the air, celebrating his return. In the days that followed, the *Boston Gazette* congratulated him for delivering the news "in a shorter time than could be expected at this season of the year."[3] Revere's acclaim was rising. Following his return, patriots even started singing the tavern ditty about his part in the Tea Party:

> Our Warren's there, and bold Revere,
> With hands to do and words to cheer,
> For liberty and laws;
> Our country's "braves" and firm defenders
> Shall ne'er be left by true North-Enders
> Fighting Freedom's cause!
> Then rally boys, and hasten on
> To meet our chiefs at the Green Dragon.[4]

But there was no time to bask in the glory or glory in the adulation. Amid the celebration, Paul was back to work the day after his arrival, guarding the tea ships to make sure that a roused and rowdy populace did no damage to the vessels.[5]

And within a week he was back to work in his shop as well. In January 1774 Revere's friend, publisher Isaiah Thomas, launched the *Royal American Magazine*. Paul had illustrated another of Thomas's publications, the scrappy *Massachusetts Spy*, for several years. But the *Royal American Magazine* courted a more highbrow audience, and Thomas advertised that it would feature Revere's "elegant Engravings." In time those included everything from political cartoons, portraits of Adams and Hancock, naturalist illustrations of beehives and cobras, an elaborate sea-and-landscape of Boston, even a pastoral romantic of a woman sheltering her sleeping companion from a thunderstorm by pulling the hem of her skirts over his head.[6]

He also engraved a plate for a new two-volume edition of the voyages of the famed explorer of the South Pacific, Captain James Cook. The illustration shows more than a dozen islanders under a veranda, watching two women and a man dance while two men beat drums and another blows a woodwind. Unlike his run-in with Pelham, there's no record that he got in trouble for pinching his design from another engraver, which he did.[7] The print from which he worked was sent by New York publisher James Rivington. He hired Revere through their mutual acquaintance, bookseller Henry Knox. It's not Paul's best work, but he was perhaps rushed more than usual. Said Rivington in his letter to Knox, "Enclosed is a Print which I desire you will immediately employ Mr. Riviere to engrave with all ability in his power and to let it be done as soon as possible. . . . I beg his best Execution and speedy dispatch of it," which only shows that the wait-and-then-hurry-up reversal common to publishers is nearly as old as it is universal.[8]

Along with all the engraving work, Paul recommenced his usual goldsmith activity of repair and crafting. He even did some dental work. But now that the tea had been dunked, there was none of the political lull that followed the Boston Massacre acquittals.

Politics was newly hot, hot, hot. While the more moderate John Hancock's radical ardor cooled following the collapse of the nonimportation agreement, the events surrounding the Tea Party seemed to light his fire again. On 5 March 1774 he, in fact, gave the annual massacre oration, and it was a doozy. Benjamin Church helped write the speech, and it stung the ears of the listeners:

Let every parent tell the shameful story to his listening children till tears of pity glisten in their eyes, and boiling passion shakes their tender frames; and whilst the anniversary of that ill-fated night is kept a jubilee in the grim court of pandaemonium [hell], let all America join in one common prayer to Heaven, that the inhuman, unprovok'd murders of the Fifth of March 1770 . . . may ever stand in history without a parallel.[9]

About the same time more East India Company tea arrived. Not as much as before, but it met with the same fate, every leafy clump chucked into the harbor.

Another arrival came as well in the form of a new recommendation about patriot communications. Perhaps learning the lesson of Bernard's and Hutchinson's letters, the colonists realized they should form their own postal service to keep loyalist eyes off their mail and also further link the colonies by expanding the free flow of information. Revere wrote back to Lamb about the idea.

"I am highly pleased about the plan," he said. "I think it is one of the greatest strokes that our Enemies have mett with (except the late affairs of the Tea) since 1768. . . ." The Boston Committee of Correspondence approved of the plan, along with "all our true sons," said Revere. The committee "wrote to all the committees of correspondence between here & Falmouth stating the case and as soon as they hear from them if they adopt the plan (which no doubt but they will) measures will be taken to carry it imeaditly into Execution."[10]

He also told him about Boston's second Tea Party: "& should 500 more come, it will go the same way. . . ." He then told him that more tea was heading to New York. "I expect," said Revere, "to hear a good account of it."[11]

In February, General Thomas Gage was in England. He wrote Thomas Hutchinson to let him know about Massachusetts' request that he be removed from power and also about the harm done him by the publishing of his letters. He said no one took the request much seriously and said that most defended his honor. But the Tea Party precipitated an ominous comment: "People talk more seriously than ever about America: that the cricis is come, when the Provinces must bee either British Colonies, or independent and separate States. What will be done, nobody I believe can yet tell. . . . Nothing can be fixed."[12] By fixed he meant "certain," but the double entendre to "repaired" is hard to ignore.

What would be done would be known soon, and it would involve the reduction of Hutchinson and the increase of Gage.

While Revere's letter was finding its way to Lamb through the post and long before word of the second Tea Party had reached Britain, Parliament passed what patriots dubbed the Intolerable Acts, a series of enactments that, among other things, forced the close of Boston Harbor, took the vote for the Governor's Council away from the General Court, moved the General Court proceedings out of Boston to Salem, and forbade town meetings unless approved by the governor. To make bad matters worse, Hutchinson would no longer be governor. The Crown requested him home and appointed General Gage to be governor of the colony.

The news came 10 May. Gage arrived just three days later. Boston patriots were outraged. The Committee of Correspondence met and arranged for Revere to send the news to their sister colonies.

Saturday, 14 May, and Revere was on the road. He carried with him new nonimportation proposals from Sam Adams and copies of the Port Act bordered in black and decorated with a skull and crossbones, undoubtedly of his own making. Above the skull he placed a crown, below the skull a liberty cap. Gage's letter said that the "Provinces must bee either British Colonies, or independent and separate States." His presence in Boston was to force the former. Revere's illustration suggested the other—there was only death between Britain and America.[13] The broadsides he would leave in towns and hamlets as he rode, alerting the countryside to the goings-on.

He also carried private letters, among them one from Thomas Young to his and Revere's mutual friend John Lamb: "My worthy friend, Revere, again revisits you. No man of his rank and opportunities in life deserves better of the community. Steady, vigorous, sensible and persevering."[14] There's some condescension in those words. Young was a doctor and a man of the "better sort." Revere was an artisan, of the middling sort. But regardless of the presumptions, Revere was growing in stature and importance in the patriot movement.

The journey was much more agreeable than the one back in December. With the last of the winter snows gone since late March, the oaks, elms latticed with their verandas of foliage. The maples thickly leaved. The slender birches. Blooms were out on the pear and apple trees, grasses grew up tall and lush, and the shade cooled him after miles of hard riding.

New Yorkers got word of the Boston Port Act around the same time Boston did (but not Boston's response—they would have to wait on Revere for that). They rushed to show support. They sent copies of their resolutions to back Boston with a rider of their own, John Ludlow, who left New York on 14 May.[15] Ludlow told the villages he passed as he rode about the Port Act and New York's support. Finally, as one apocryphal story has it, the two riders met just off the road at a spring outside Providence, Rhode Island. Surrounded by lush, late spring foliage, the men watered their horses and ate lunch together. Then: back on the horses and back down the road, Ludlow pressing toward Boston, Revere toward New York. No rest for the weary.[16]

When he arrived in New York, the patriots reiterated their support already en route if not yet arrived by the hand of Ludlow. Then Revere was back on his steed and making for Philadelphia. The news was the same in the City of Brotherly Love. Philadelphia patriots met to consider "the execrable Port Bill." They committed to stand with Boston "to the last extremity." They also advised, delivered by the hands of Revere, instituting "a General Congress of all the Colonies."[17] That hadn't been done since the Stamp Act Congress. And it seemed such a Continental Congress might really work. By month's end, Revere was back with news that besides New York and Philadelphia, Rhode Island and Connecticut were in their camp.[18]

Revere returned home to a galvanized city. Parliament's impositions left patriots with the feeling that, as one man put it, London could now "d—n us whenever they please," regardless of their guilt.[19] Faced with Parliament's firm hand, more than a hundred Boston merchants promised to pay for the tea while lobbying the town meeting to submit to the Port Act. Nothing doing. The town meeting rejected the merchants, backed further boycotts, and defended the actions of the Committee of Correspondence. Meanwhile Sam Adams ran with the general congress notion and put forth a resolution in the General Court for a Continental Congress. The General Court signed on; the new body would meet in Philadelphia on the first of September.[20] The same day the patriots in the assembly voted for the congress, Gage proved the necessity of it. He formally dissolved the General Court, as Bernard had also done. But no one went along with it, least of all Paul Revere.

In June Revere etched a shocking print that described what was happening to America. America is represented as a half-disrobed woman in a near rape. Held down hands and feet by a law-yer and a "gentleman,"

The Crown's enforcer, General Thomas Gage.
Library of Congress.

177

another man with a copy of the Boston Port Bill poking from his jacket pocket holds her by the throat with one hand and forces tea down her gullet with the other, while she spews it back. The man holding her feet looks up her dress with an evil grin on his face while a man with a sword—"Military Law"—oversees the injustice. The goddess Liberty is in the background. All she can do is hide her face for the shame of it all.[21] But America wasn't going to go along with the injustice. She would resist.

Gage clamped down. After he dissolved the General Court, he banned other patriot gatherings. In both cases the people ignored him. They held illegal town meetings as well as other confabs, and patriot groups and gatherings continued in the town and through the Committees of Correspondence.[22] When the town clergy met with Gage to appoint a day of fasting and prayer and he declined, they did it without him.[23] And while the port was closed, the only ships coming in and out were those bringing more troops. With merchants of either patriot or loyalist stripes unable to land goods, sympathetic citizens as far away as Connecticut sent grain and livestock into the town.[24]

The patriots found other ways to resist. Mobs in the outlying counties harassed Crown officials. Several county courts were prevented from operating. Gage had to send troops to the countryside to protect the officers.

The resistance continued right under Gage's nose. Two days before the Continental Congress was to commence in Philadelphia, the Boston Superior Court of Judicature convened. Chief Justice Peter Oliver, his fellow justices, a bevy of attorneys, the sheriff and his deputies processed from the Town House down Queen Street to the courthouse. The justices and others took their seats. Gage joined them. With initial formalities out of the way, the court moved to impanel the grand jury. The foreman was named. He rose when called but refused to be sworn in. The other jurors as well, Paul among them.[25]

Goliath was facing an ever-growing array of Davids.

Two days after Revere and the other grand jurors refused to serve, Thursday, 1 September, Gage dispatched troops to seize gunpowder stores in Charlestown. They left Boston by boat at 4:30 in the morning, landed in Charlestown, marched to the powder house, seized more than two hundred barrels of gunpowder, returned to their boats, and deposited the load at Castle Island. The whole operation took about five hours.[26]

The real fireworks happened the next day, when a near uprising occurred. Much of the earlier political struggles centered in Boston and involved their bad behavior. But the Intolerable Acts and the abrogation of the Massachusetts charter agitated all the counties of the colony. On 2 September the militia—minutemen—turned out, and despite intolerable heat there were mass demonstrations in Cambridge. They forced the resignations of several of the Crown-appointed members of the Governor's Council.

Revere wrote Lamb to tell him:

Dear S[R], I embrace this opportunity to inform you, that we are in Spirits, tho' in a Garrison; the Spirit of Liberty never was higher than at present; the Troops have the horrors amazingly, by reason of some late movements of our friends in the Country the week past, our new fangled Councellors are resigning their places every Day; our Justices of the Courts, who now hold their Commissions during the pleasure of his Majesty, or the Governor, cannot git a Jury that will act with them, in short the Tories are giving way every where in our Province.[27]

The letter was humble. Revere never mentioned his part in rejecting service on the grand jury. It was also perhaps overly optimistic. If the patriots were to reestablish the self-rule they were accustomed to, it would require a lot more work. Revere would find out soon enough, as he was one of the chief actors.

The uprising accomplished one thing; it put the fear of God in Gage. He moved immediately to fortify Boston Neck against possible insurrection.

One week after his letter to Lamb, Revere rode again, this time a three-hundred-mile trek to Philadelphia to deliver the Suffolk Resolves to the Continental Congress. He arrived on 16 September. The delegates read the resolves the following day before all those assembled inside Liberty Hall. They said among other things that Massachusetts owed "no obedience" to the Port Act or Massachusetts Government Act, "but that they should be rejected as the attempts of a wicked administration to enslave America." They also suggested that there be total tax resistance until the "constitutional" government was restored, that the courts be ignored, and that they opposed "all routs, riots, or licentious attacks upon property of any persons whatsoever . . . our conduct shall be such as to merit the approbation of the wise, and the admiration of the brave and free of every age and of every country."[28] The assembly clapped. Some even cried.[29]

Paul set out on the eighteenth and arrived back in Boston, Friday evening, 23 September. The word he carried—the Bay Colony had the full support of the Continental Congress. He was back in the saddle and quick out of town less than a week later, on 29 September. Then a week later he rode again, carrying fresh news to Philadelphia. This time he stayed a while. He didn't depart again for Boston until 11 October. In all this Revere was the vital link between the patriots in Congress and those in Boston; the latter, Warren wrote Sam Adams, were "rapacious for the intelligence brought from the Congress by Mr. Revere. . . ."[30]

Once back in Boston that fall, Revere and some thirty other mechanics formed a clandestine intelligence ring in Boston to keep track of the comings and goings of both British soldiers and the local loyalists. They met—where else?—at the Green Dragon. "We were so careful that our meetings should be kept secret, that every time we met, every person swore upon the Bible that he would not discover any of our transactions but to Messrs Hancock, Adams, Doctors Warren, Church and one or two more."[31]

But somebody was spilling the beans. As Paul later said, "About November, when things began to grow Serious, a Gentleman who had Conections with the Tory party, but was a Whig at heart, acquainted me, that our meetings were discovered, and mentioned the identical words that were spoken among us the Night before." They moved their meeting locations. But it did no good—"here we found that all our transactions were communicated to Governor Gage. . . . It was then a common opinion, that there was a Traytor in the provincial Congress, and that Gage was posessed of all their Secrets."[32] Secret meetings. Spies. Word of a Judas in their midst. If war wasn't already under way, it was fast coming.

With the seizure of the Charlestown powder fresh in mind, on 8 December a committee of the Massachusetts Provincial Congress reported "that gunpowder is an article of such importance, that every man among us who loves his country, must wish the establishment of manufactories for that purpose." The committee recommended repairing several of the derelict powder mills in the colony.[33] No one took them up on the offer. Apparently it was more effective for the moment to steal the king's powder.

It was as a representative of the Committee of Safety that on 13 December Revere rode to patriots in Portsmouth,

New Hampshire, warning them that Gage had designs on the powder at Fort William and Mary. Hearing the news, the militia snapped into action and seized the fort before the soldiers could, gaining control of the coveted and much-needed gunpowder stores.

That wasn't the end of the matter. Gage soon set his eyes on Concord and the powder stores there.

Revere's reputation soared for the patriots in the northern colonies and sank for the loyalists. Gage was aware of his activities, though his name appears only as "P:__ R:__" in his correspondence.[34] And his feats were noted as far away as London, where a paper identified him in November 1774 as "Express from Congress of Boston to Philadelphia."[35] Paul's cousin John Rivoire back in Guernsey even took note of that.[36] But for all his growing fame, Paul's most famous ride was still to come.

CHAPTER 17

Ride!

*In which our hero plays spy before General Gage
makes his move on Lexington and Concord,
whereupon he sets two lights blazing
in a high spire before riding to warn his
compatriots and roust the sleeping countryside
as dawn breaks on open war.*

Paul Revere turned forty on 21 December 1774, just a fortnight following the birth of Joshua, his first child with new wife, Rachel. The littlest Revere was baptized at West Church on the eleventh. Despite the tumults, Paul's engraving, goldsmithing, and dentistry business drew almost £121 by year's end.[1] The significance of such personal milestones and professional achievements, however, changed now that Boston was in the wrench of General Gage and his soldiers.

Gage's powder seizures and troop mobilizations signaled to patriots both in Boston and the surrounding countryside that their new governor meant to put a tight kink in their activities. It was certain that he would act again. *Where* and *why* were no mystery—Concord, to seize the munitions stored there by the militia. *When* was the question. It was a time, as one man remembered, of "dread Suspense."[2]

The Sons of Liberty, Revere among them, kept their eyes peeled. "In the Winter, towards the Spring, we frequently took Turns, two and two, to Watch the Soldiers," he said, "By patroling the Streets all night." The intelligence that they gathered and pooled, all the whispers, rumors, and reports, began to firm up and reveal the shape of Gage's plan. The general had been sending his men into the countryside and drilling on the Common to accustom the townsfolk to redcoat activity. But he turned up the heat too fast, and after an abrupt and splashy repositioning of troop transport boats in the harbor on 7 April, the frog jumped out of the kettle.[3]

Joseph Warren was one of the last of the patriot leaders still in Boston on Saturday, 8 April. Most of the others, like Samuel Adams and John Hancock, were at the Provincial Congress then meeting in Concord.[4] Warren sent Revere to warn the patriots at Concord about the troop transports and that it appeared as if Gage would deploy his redcoats the very next day. Revere delivered Warren's message, and the townsfolk began squirreling the supplies elsewhere.[5] But Warren and Revere were wrong on the timing. Gage was coiled, yes, twitching even, but not yet ready to strike. Not yet.

In a week things would change.

On Saturday, 15 April, Gage heard from London that reinforcements were coming. In the same secret missive came direct orders to seize all military supplies and "to arrest the principal actors and abettors in the Provincial Congress," that is, men like Adams and Hancock.[6]

Gage started preparations immediately. It was "about 12 oClock at Night" that "the Boats belonging to the Transports were all launched, and carried under the Sterns of the Men of War. (They had previously been hauled up and repaired)," Paul recalled. Additionally Revere and his intelligence team "found that the Grenadiers and light Infantry were all taken off duty." As he summed it up, "From these movements, we expected something serious was [to] be transacted."[7]

The next day, 16 April, was Easter, but Gage spent less time contemplating the Resurrection than he did another important message that had arrived, this one from his spy inside the Provincial Congress.

The message said that the congress had authorized raising a New England army before recessing on 15 April. At that point, Gage needed no further proof that the colonials were in open rebellion, but the recess was valuable information. With the congress adjourned, the only acting patriot government was the Committee of Safety in Cambridge. Now was the time. A move against Concord couldn't be better timed, as far as the spy was concerned. "A sudden blow struck now," he wrote, "would oversett all their plans."[8]

While the spy's letter made its way into town, Paul made his way out. He took a boat across the Charles River to Charlestown. With the Provincial Congress on recess and the Continental Congress soon to convene, Adams and Hancock decided to stay under the roof of Rev. Jonas Clark of Lexington. They didn't need to know about the orders for arrest to know that they were *personae non grata* in Gage's Boston. Revere updated them of the troop movements.

Then, with his mission accomplished, Revere took a precaution on his way back that later, through the pen of poet Henry Wadsworth Longfellow, inked him an indelible mark in the American imagination. Should the patriots in the country need warning again, Paul planned on making his way back across the river to Charlestown, but it was always possible—maybe even likely—that the redcoats would stop boat traffic and prevent him from getting across. What then? Should Revere or another messenger be stopped, the patriots across the river would need a signal from Boston if the troops were moving out and by what route. "I returned at Night thro Charlestown," Paul recounted; "there I agreed with a Col. [William] Conant, and some other Gentlemen, that if the British went out by Water, we would shew two Lanthorns in the North Church Steeple; and if by Land, one, as a Signal; for we were apprehensive it would be difficult to Cross the Charles River, or git over Boston Neck."[9]

The North Church, the same church at which the boy

Paul learned to ring the bells, sported the tallest steeple in town and was even used by seamen as a landmark when entering the harbor.[10] They should be able to see it in Charlestown, no trouble, an assumption they'd be able to put to the test very soon.

Despite Gage's every effort to bottle the news under a tight cork and thick wax, it leaked out. From muffled lips to wide ears it spread, heading around corners and through alleyways back to Warren and Revere, who collected and weighed every utterance.[11] The fact seemed plain: the troops were mobilizing.

It was Tuesday, 18 April. After the false alarm ten days prior, Warren wanted confirmation before he acted. He kept a well-placed, confidential source for just such purposes, one he used only in the most needful of circumstances, somebody close to General Gage himself. It was dangerous for both Warren and the contact, but it was now or never. Out went the request. Would the answer come in time? Warren waited, hoping, fearing. And then—*yes*. The source confirmed it. Troops were marching that night to destroy the powder stores at Concord and to arrest Adams and Hancock at Lexington.[12] Warren had to warn them. He sent for Revere.

Paul was in his home when he heard the rap on the door. It was late, sometime between nine and ten o'clock. A messenger greeted him at the door and told him that Warren required him. Revere took off for his friend's house several blocks away on Hanover. Once there, Warren told Paul his mission and said that another rider, William Dawes, was already en route over Boston Neck with the same news. In case troops on the road intercepted one messenger, he hoped the other would make it through.

Paul left. Earlier in the day he'd made arrangements for his friend, church sexton Robert Newman, to display the lanterns in the steeple of the North Church; now he made for Newman's house to let him know it was time to hoist the lights. With Newman on the job, Paul then turned home and grabbed his boots and frock before ankling it up north where he hid a small rowboat at the ready.[13]

Eyes in Charlestown were fixed on the soaring steeple of North Church, backlit by the nearly full rising moon. The moment they saw the twin gleams from the spire, the patriots scurried, sending a rider to Cambridge to alert the Committee of Safety and rushing to make preparations.[14]

Cambridge would know soon enough, even without the rider. While Paul and the others raced, the redcoats on the Common began making their way aboard the boats en route to the Cambridge side of the river to begin the march to Lexington.

As Paul and the other patriots had assumed, getting across

the Charles River was no easy chore. Gage determined to throw a wet blanket on the whole of Boston. The military had stopped all river traffic at 9:00 p.m. and had seized not only the ferries but also anything else that floated. For those few boats that evaded and avoided seizure, like Paul's, Gage went one step further and anchored the massive sixty-four-gun man-of-war, *Somerset*, smack-dab in the middle of the passage. And there it was, looming, swaying, threatening, as two of Paul's friends dipped muffled oars into the waves and drove his little skiff ever closer through the lapping waves, clearing the hulking ship hidden from sight by a shadow of the rising moon.[15]

Paul put to shore near the Charlestown Battery and hustled into town. He found Colonel Conant and his men. Revere "told them what was Acting, and went to git me a Horse." While a big brown mare owned by the Congregational church deacon John Larkin was being readied, another man just in from Lexington a few hours before told Paul about a team of soldiers on horseback. They were "all well mounted, and armed, going up the Road." More of Gage's precautions. Not that his others had served him very well so far. It was now about eleven. Paul swung into the saddle and rode over Charlestown Neck.[16]

The road before him was simple enough. Once over the Neck, he'd hook a left on the road to Cambridge, then a right and on up to Lexington. He set an even pace, big glossy moon lighting his path all the way—no point rushing headlong into a patrol or pooping out Larkin's horse halfway there—and clopped his way through the Charlestown

Common, an unpopulated stretch of scrubland, salt marshes, and clay pits between the Charles and Mystic rivers.[17]

Before he'd cleared the Common, Revere saw them— two riders in long, blue cloaks at a squeeze point in the road, shrouded in pitchy shadows of an overhanging tree. Paul was nearly on them before he realized. "I was near enough to see their Holsters, and cockades," he said. Out

Paul Revere on horseback, waking up the countryside.
Library of Congress.

192

from cover they lunged, their beasts surging beneath them, as one came straight at him and the other tried to head him off. Paul spun Larkin's horse and pushed back up the road toward Charlestown Neck and then leftward for the Medford Road. This route was longer, but it was better than getting caught. Had Dawes met similar trouble in his journey? Did he make it through? Paul evaded his pursuers, one of whom got slogged down in a clay pit. He rode on through Medford, where he woke the captain of the militia. "[A]nd after that," he said, "I alarmed almost every House, till I got to Lexington."[18]

Revere arrived in Lexington about midnight. He made for Rev. Jonas Clark's straightaway. When he arrived, he found a guard—one of several watching the house—posted at the door. Paul asked to go inside. The guard refused, saying that everyone had just bedded down for the night and requested that there be no noise.

"Noise!" said an excited Revere. "You'll have noise enough before long. The regulars are coming out." The guard knew well enough that regulars meant redcoats.[19]

Paul's voice was as unmistakable as it was loud. From inside, Hancock and the others could hear him. Up flew the windows. "Come in, Revere!" barked Hancock. "We're not afraid of *you*."[20]

In he went and, as he later recounted, "told them my errand." The whole house was up and buzzing now. Troops on their way! Arrests planned! Munitions to be destroyed!

It's all beginning. Paul then asked about William Dawes. Had he come? He should have arrived already.

No. No sign of him.

He told them about the soldiers on the road and mentioned that he must have been intercepted. But then after, Paul had been there just a half hour, Dawes arrived. For Paul's later start and troubles on the road, he proved the quicker messenger. With the news delivered, the two sat down for some well-earned refreshment—probably at Buckman Tavern right off the Lexington Green where many members of the militia were also stationed—before saddling up again and heading to Concord to warn the people there. Other messengers were already being sent out from Lexington to Cambridge, Bedford, and other communities.[21]

As Revere and Dawes left town, a young doctor, Samuel Prescott, rode up behind them. He'd been in town, courting his girl, and was now heading back to Concord. Revere mentioned the roaming redcoats he'd heard about in Charlestown and those he met on the road. There were likely more between them and Concord. Rather than rushing ahead, Paul suggested that they "alarm all the Inhabitents till [they] got to Concord." That way, if they were intercepted, the news could still get to Concord. Prescott approved and joined their mission. He was known by all the locals, he said, and could lend credit to the news of Revere and Dawes.[22]

The journey from Lexington to Concord was about six miles. They'd gone just three when trouble started. Dawes and Prescott were rousing a dwelling. Paul was up the road about a hundred yards. And then he saw them. Redcoats! It was the same as before, two riders hidden in the shadows. But this time Revere had an edge—two companions of his own. Paul turned and yelled to Dawes and Prescott. But as they rode up from behind, Revere found himself—"in an Instant"—surrounded by four other redcoat riders with swords and pistols.[23]

"G—d d—n you!" they shouted. "Stop! If you go an Inch further, you are a dead Man."[24]

Dying would have been extremely inconvenient, sure, but Revere wasn't about to stop. Prescott was now at his side, their horses edgy, shifting, and stamping. The soldiers had taken down part of the roadside fence and were pushing Revere and Prescott into the pasture, guns brandished and menacing. "[W]e attempted to git thro them," said Paul, "but they kept before us, and swore if we did not turn in to that pasture, they would blow our brains out."[25]

The soldiers edged them into the pasture, but then Prescott spied an out. He bolted, jumped a low stone wall, and made for Concord.[26]

Dawes, meanwhile, flew toward a nearby farmhouse, with soldiers hot on his tail. There was no getting away. He came to an abrupt stop at the house, slapped his leather breeches, and blurted the bluff of his life. "Halloo, boys!" he shouted to the house, loud enough for his pursuers to hear. "I've got two of 'em!" The soldiers bought it and took off, leaving him free to escape.[27]

Paul hoped for similar getaway. Always with an eye

for the main chance, he spotted a nearby forested area, spurred Larkin's horse, and thundered away. But then out came more redcoats. Six riders converged on him, forced him to stop, and ordered him out of the saddle.[28]

With Paul's feet on the sod, the apparent commander of the group started pumping him for information.

What's your name?

Paul answered.

Are you an express?

Paul said yes.

What time did you leave Boston?

Paul gave the time and threw in a bluff. He "added, that their troops had catched aground in passing the River, and that There would be five hundred Americans there in a short time, for I had alarmed the Country all the way up." He knew about the alarm, of course, but had no idea of the troops getting hung up before landing in Cambridge.[29] Sounded good, though.

The inquest stopped, and the commander turned away and rode to the other group who had originally stopped Paul. Then they all spun back around and rode to where Paul was standing in custody. One Major Edward Mitchell wasted no time. He "clapped his pistol to my head, called me by name, and told me he was going to ask me some questions, and if I did not give him true answers, he would blow my brains out."[30]

Mitchell might have been vicious, but he wasn't very original. His questions were pretty much the same as those of the first officer. Paul regurgitated his previous answers before Mitchell ordered him searched for weapons (Paul rode unarmed that night, which might have saved his life) and then back in the saddle. Once Paul was astride Larkin's horse, Mitchell seized the reins from him.[31]

"[B]y God Sir you are not to ride with reins I assure you," he said and then added, "We are now going toward your friends, and if you attempt to run, or we are insulted, we will blow your Brains out."[32]

"I told him he might do as he pleased," recounted Paul.[33]

So they made for the road and re-formed, directing Paul to take the lead, ahead of a few other prisoners. And then back to Lexington.

They moved fast, and the troops' tongues kept pace with the clopping horses. "They very often insulted me," recounted Revere, "calling me d—ned Rebel &c. &c."

After about a mile, Mitchell placed Revere in another's charge and ordered him to shoot Paul in the head if he tried to escape. After another mile and some distance, a gun was heard—thankfully not one aimed at Paul's head. It seemed to come from near the town. Mitchell asked what was going on. Paul told him that the shot was to alert the countryside. Mitchell immediately unsaddled and unbridled the other prisoners' horses, drove them away, and then set the men at liberty. No such luck for Revere. "I asked the Major to dismiss me," said Paul. Nothing doing, said Mitchell.[34]

As the group closed in on Lexington, a fresh chorus of shots rang out from the town, probably a militia alarm from Buckman Tavern. Mitchell didn't want to ride into a hornets' nest, but that's how it was starting to look. How close is it to Cambridge? he asked Paul. Were there any other roads? Then he turned to the man in whose charge he left Revere and asked him if his mount was tired. The man answered yes, and then Paul suddenly found himself without an animal. He was ordered out of the saddle, and the soldier mounted Larkin's mare before the whole troop left Paul alone, free, in the road while they took off into the night.[35]

Paul made his way across a graveyard and some pastures back into town. He found Adams and Hancock and told them everything that had happened. This was no place for a couple of men now officially wanted for treason. The patriotic pair hightailed it to the nearby town of Woburn, and Paul went with them to make sure they arrived safely.

When Paul arrived back at Lexington a short time later, just before dawn, the troops were on the edge of town. Riders came in saying that they would be marching into town any moment. Hancock's clerk, John Lowell, asked Paul to help him with a certain case of documents and other papers stored in his room at the tavern. They were Hancock's and likely contained enough incriminating evidence to hang half the patriots in Massachusetts for treason, not least of all himself. The chest was large

The Battle at Lexington.
Library of Congress.

and required both men to hoist and carry. From the bed-room window, the two could see the redcoats converging on the town, "upon a full March." Revere and Lowell, their ungainly load swinging between them, left as quick as they could and went straight for Clark's house—right through the lines of the amassing militia, about fifty men in total.[36] Then as Paul remembered:

> When we had got about 100 Yards from the meeting-House the British Troops appeard on both Sides of the Meeting-House. In their Front was an Officer on Horse back. They made a Short Halt; when I saw, and heard, a Gun fired, which appeared to be a Pistol. Then I could distinguish two Guns, and then a Continual roar of Musquetry; When we made off with the Trunk.[37]

War had begun.

The fighting lasted all day, the outnumbered and fatigued redcoats finally making the long march back to Boston in the afternoon. They marched for hours, all the while, militiamen sniped at them from the woods and swarmed on the beleaguered redcoats like hornets.

CHAPTER 18

Betrayal

*In which the patriots are exiled in
their own lands and rally against
the redcoats, while our hero is rejoined by
his dear wife and family as the treachery
of the Revolution's first Judas is exposed.*

When Revere arrived at Hastings House in Cambridge, Joseph Warren was already there. The Committee of Safety was now meeting at the house, and Warren, president of the body, had work for his friend Paul. "He engaged me as a Messinger," Paul recounted, "to do the out of doors business for that committee."[1] The gig paid four shillings a day.[2]

Benjamin Church, who'd been at the Provincial Congress, was there as well and showed Paul blood splatters on his socks, "which he said spirited on him from a Man who

201

was killed near him, as he was urging the Militia on." Paul was impressed with the way he'd put his life at "risqué."[3]

Church now seemed adamant about living on the edge. On Friday, 22 April, the committee was meeting after a long day of taking depositions from witnesses to the fight at Lexington and Concord, including one from Paul.[4] It was sunset. Suddenly Church stood up and announced he was sneaking back into Boston.

"Are you serious, Dr. Church?" asked Warren. "[T]hey will Hang you if they catch you in Boston."

"I am serious, and am determined to go at all adventures."

The whole room stared in disbelief. There was much discussion, but finally Warren relented. "If you are determined, let us make some business for you."[5]

The job was to procure medical supplies for the wounded officers. For a doctor, that should be reasonable cover—and the Brits would be unlikely to molest someone on a medical mission. At least not much.

Paul, meanwhile, was anxious to hear from Rachel. Revere biographer Esther Forbes suggests that Paul sneaked into town the day before and met with Rachel, their parting understanding being that she would secure him some cash. Revere saw his chance. Church could pick up whatever Rachel was able to gather and bring it back for him. Paul made the arrangement with Church that same night. The next day, both were off on their respective errands—Paul, delivering messages; Church, taking his life in his hands.[6]

Church was back by Sunday evening, and contra Warren, his neck had been noosed by nothing more dangerous than collar and cravat. After Church debriefed the committee about the state of affairs in Boston, Paul pulled him aside. As Revere recalled, "He said, that as soon as he got to their lines on Boston Neck, they made him a prisoner, and carried him to General Gage, where He was examined, and then He was sent to Gould's Barracks, and was not suffered to go home but once."[7] And the money from Rachel? It made sense that Church couldn't get it from her if he was under arrest while he was in town. He didn't even ask him about it. For now, Paul would have to make do with his messenger's wage.

In the meantime, the colonists readied for the siege of Boston. Colonel Richard Gridley led the effort. Revere, who had served under Gridley back in 1756 during the French and Indian War, sought an artillery commission but was denied. There were a few things going against him. For starters, Paul wasn't a gentleman—not in the sense that mattered. The rules of class and distinction were often bent in Boston but not enough to get him around this limitation. Not yet. Next, nothing came of his previous service under Gridley, so there was nothing now to recommend him.

There were also some Masonic hurdles involved. Revere was an Ancient Mason, Gridley a Modern. The rift between the two groups was still unhealed and its effects long felt—brotherhood meant something, but it only went so far.

Worse for Paul, the only other commander who could help Revere get the commission was William Burbeck, the same William Burbeck with whom the Masons of St. Andrew's fought a few years prior regarding their charter. Recourse to him was no recourse at all. In short, there was no commission quick in coming for Paul Revere. He had to content himself with "out of doors work" for Warren and the Committee of Safety.[8] But he wasn't content to do it alone. He wanted Rachel and his children by his side.

Paul and Rachel exchanged urgent letters at this time, trying to make arrangements for the family to leave Boston. "My Dear Girl," he wrote:

> I am glad you have got yourself ready. If you find that you cannot easily get a pass for the Boat, I would have you get a pass for yourself and children and effects. Send the most valuable first. I mean that you should send Beds enough for yourself and Children, my chest, your trunk, with Books, Cloaths &c to the ferry tell the ferryman they are mine. I will provide a house here where to put them & will be here to receive them.[9]

The only person to stay back was Paul Jr. To him, Paul wrote:

My Son.

It is now in your power to be serviceable to me, your Mother and yourself. I beg you will keep yourself at home or where your Mother sends you. Don't you come away till I send you word. When you bring anything to the ferry tell them it is mine & mark it with my name.

Your loving Father
"P. R."[10]

There was additional correspondence full of discussion about passes, bribes, and the like, but eventually by mid-May the Revere family was on the other side of the Charles River, excluding Paul Jr., who was left behind to guard the shop and might have considered the British a welcome swap for the crammed quarters of the house that his father secured in Watertown.[11]

There was a good deal of traffic like this around Boston initially. Loyalists from the countryside streaming in. Patriots streaming out. Before leaving Boston, patriots had to surrender their arms. "It resulted in 1778 firearms, 973 bayonets, 634 pistols, and 38 blunderbusses," writes Esther Forbes, "which gives an idea how heavily armed the average citizen was in those days." To help get mom and siblings out, Paul Jr. turned over two of the family's muskets.[12]

The standard picture of displaced populations holds true. Most of usual life was disrupted or put on hold, while people figured out how to make do with the new reality of war. One of the hardest things to manage when all the usual patterns of commerce had stopped was a wage. Paul no doubt asked Rachel about the funds she was supposed to have sent.

Didn't you receive it?

No.

I gave it to Dr. Church.

And where now was Dr. Church? The Provincial Congress ordered him to Philadelphia on 16 May to liaise with the Continental Congress on the question of who should lead the New England armies.[13] So he wasn't around to ask. But no worries. Paul was resourceful; he'd already begun figuring out how to make money through other channels.

Even in the most literal sense.

That same month, the Provincial Congress authorized Revere to engrave and print notes of credit—paper money. Paul's father had learned the art from his master, John Coney. Now it was the younger Revere's turn. Paul adorned his first run of bills with a foliated frame containing a buskined patriot in a toga and robe with a staff and liberty cap under another frame in which—hearkening back to the original wealth of the colony—sits a codfish. As the colonists had discovered through hard experience, paper money is dangerous stuff and easily used to the betterment of some and ruination of many. The congress was concerned and required Revere to hide his engraving press "when he is absent from it" and also to turn over the plates when the full run of bills was done. For his efforts, Paul was paid £50.[14] (It's got to be a unique feeling, knowing exactly how much you're worth in money that you just printed.)

The money Paul printed was used in large part to fund the war effort, particularly to pay the soldiers who were staked out around Boston for the siege. The Brits were holed up inside the town like rats in a tight corner. Their only chance at this point was to strike out and gain strategic positions south in Dorchester and north in Charlestown. If they could manage that, the redcoats stood a fighting chance. If not, the colonists could swoop into the same places and

Joseph Warren before the battle at Breed's Hill.
Library of Congress.

position cannon on the surrounding hills and then fire into the heart of the town—the same way the French battered Fort William Henry to smithereens with mortar fire back in the French and Indian War. Game over.

On 15 June, the patriots heard that Gage was making his play for Dorchester and Charlestown. The next day, the Committee of Safety sent a thousand men to protect the towns. Joseph Warren was among them. Before heading into battle, he tucked a small Psalter into his coat. They went to work immediately, but the real action started the following day when the redcoats attacked Charlestown. About 2:00 p.m. 17 June, British General William Howe sent a red wave crashing up the slopes of Breed's Hill. The Americans, like breakers, repulsed them. Howe regrouped his men and sent them into the fire once more. The Americans repulsed them again. It was now close to 5:00 p.m. Howe pulled his men together again and sent them up the hill. But one thing had changed. This time the Americans were out of powder. The red wave overran the hill, and the colonists sounded retreat. Warren waited on the hill, waited till the last moment. He finally turned, but it was too late. A lead ball blasted through his skull and killed him instantly. The loyalists lost a noble foe, the patriots an invaluable leader, and Revere a trusted friend.[15]

Not long after the tragic battle, the patriots lost another from their ranks.

Benjamin Church kept a mistress, which wasn't the first

of his follies, as it turned out; those began long before. Nonetheless, in the summer of 1775 he gave her a letter to deliver. But instead of putting it into the hands Church had directed, she gave it to a Newport, Rhode Island, baker named Godfrey Wainwood, who said he'd take care of it. He didn't. He opened it. The letter was in code. Wainwood knew something was fishy and put the missive into patriot hands and eventually all the way up the chain to George Washington, who had the woman (one contemporary referred to her as an "infamous hussey") arrested. After some resistance, she finally finked on Church, who was then taken into custody while the letter was being deciphered. Once decoded, it revealed Church's espionage efforts, information on patriot military activities and troop strengths, and the need to communicate everything in code, closing with the ominous line "Make use of every precaution or I perish."[16]

The extent of Church's treachery began tumbling out around the feet of his friends, confidants, and cobelligerents. It went back at least as far as 1772, when then Governor Hutchinson wrote to the departed Governor Bernard that "Doctor Church" is now "on the side of the Government."[17] It turns out that the good doctor kept Hutchinson apprised of patriot activity and then fell right into General Gage's pocket the moment he took over for Hutchinson. The spy ratting out Paul Revere's mechanics intelligence ring? It was Church. The spy responsible for alerting Gage to the Provincial Congress's plans? Church also. Letter followed letter, with Church exposing all their secrets.[18]

Painting of the misnamed Battle of Bunker Hill.
Library of Congress.

After the arrest, the betrayal was all the buzz. Hadn't he palled around with one British officer, Captain Price, and often dined with customs man John Robinson? Revere ran into Deacon Caleb Davis, who was in Boston the morning Church so bravely went into town "at all adventures." Davis didn't know about Price and Robinson, but he knew about a far more treacherous relation. Davis had business at the house of General Gage. When Davis arrived, Gage was already in a meeting. Davis waited for about a half hour, when who should appear? "General Gage and Dr. Church came out of a Room, discoursing together, like persons who had been long aquainted," as Revere related his conversation with Davis. Church was taken aback by seeing Davis, who said that Church seemed to go "where he pleased, while in Boston, only a Major Caine, one of

Gage's Aids, went with him." Another, "whom I could depend upon," backed up Davis's story for Revere.[19] And that Major Caine? Otherwise known as Major Maurice Cane—it was to him that Church's incriminating letter was addressed.[20]

It was some time before Church's fate was finally sifted. The patriots kept him bottled up until early 1778, when he was sent aboard a ship to the West Indies—and subsequently lost at sea.

Meanwhile, the War for Independence heated up.

CHAPTER 19

Waiting

*In which our hero fails to catch a break but ends
up putting his frustrated talents to many good
and profitable uses, including the making of
gunpowder and cannon, while the war drags on.*

The disaster at Breed's Hill and the tragic death of Joseph Warren owed in part to the patriots' lack of gunpowder. Never again.

Since the earliest days of settlement, Americans imported their powder from Britain. But now with a full-scale revolution under way, that was over. Patriots in Massachusetts turned to their jack-of-all-trades Paul Revere to solve the problem. Paul had engraved an illustration for the *Royal American Magazine* the prior year showing two men busy with the task of refining potassium nitrate, or saltpeter, the trickiest part of the process.[1] Gunpowder is about 10 percent sulfur, which is easy to come by, 15 percent charcoal, which is even easier to come by, and 75 percent saltpeter, which is not easy to come by at all. It occurs naturally as part of the decomposition process, but mass production of saltpeter didn't happen until the nineteenth century. Until then, powder makers were stuck leaching the stuff out of bird coops and barn stalls. The Americans were able to import much of their saltpeter needs from the French and Dutch, but even with all the ingredients, they were short on mills to combine them. Enter Revere. From engraving the process to making the real stuff—on 10 November 1775 the Provincial Congress sent Paul to Philadelphia to study the process from a man who operated a mill there.[2]

Ten days later Revere was in Philadelphia and ready to learn. Trouble was that the man who operated the mill was secretly a loyalist. When Paul toured his facility, the man refused to teach him anything or pass on any particular tricks of the trade. Instead he hurried Paul through the mill and forced Paul to glean what could be had through rushed observation. For Paul and his intuitive understanding of mechanics and chemistry, it was enough.[3]

Back in Massachusetts, he began work on constructing a powder mill. Others helped out. In December 1775, for instance, Sam Adams acquired the plans for a mill from a New Yorker, which he sent immediately to Revere.[4] Formal work began on a mill in Canton in February 1776. They completed it in May and turned out tons of gunpowder before the end of the war.[5]

While work progressed on the powder mill, serious shifts in the war effort happened all around, not least of which in Boston. The redcoats finally pulled out of the town in March, never to return. The patriots came again to their shops, often damaged, and their homes, typically wrecked, and tried to resume their lives. Churches were battered and torn down. The Liberty Tree was reduced to a stump.[6]

Some things required immediate attention, such as the recovery and burial of the body of the beloved Joseph Warren. A group of men, Paul among them, went across the Charles River to Charlestown on 21 March to look for his grave. It took several days, but they finally found it overgrown by a tangle of rosemary and cassia. They carefully exhumed the body, buried under several feet of soil. By then the body was grossly disfigured. Paul had to identify his departed friend by two artificial teeth and the silver wire he had placed shortly before Warren died.[7]

Warren's body was set in an elegant coffin, and a proper burial was given in the Granary burial yard, where so many of Paul's relatives laid at rest. Over his coffin Perez Morton offered the stirring words: "Shall we still contend for a connection with those who have forfeited not only every kindred claim, but even their title to humanity! forbid it [by] . . . the spirit of the immortal Warren! . . . They [the patriots departed] contended for the establishment of peace, liberty, and safety to their country; and we are unworthy to be called their countrymen, if we stop at any acquisition short of this."[8]

Revere couldn't have agreed more. In March he'd taken the rank of major in the Massachusetts State infantry and days after Warren's funeral slid into the Massachusetts State artillery train. By December he'd picked up the rank of lieutenant colonel. Paul Jr. joined as well. Just sixteen, he landed a lieutenant's commission.[9]

Revere desired a commission in the Continental army, but it wasn't coming. He had to make the most of his circumstances, which were meager indeed. With his fellows in the Bay Colony militia he patched together the necessary fortifications on Castle Island, where he took up a command.[10]

That same summer, Rachel gave birth to the couple's second child, John. With his boy only a week in the world, Paul embarked on a joint expedition of Continental and state troops to roust the British from Nantasket Harbor, where they were blocking Massachusetts Bay. The mission got off to a rough start when the artillery transports were insufficient for the job, but they made do, and Paul and his men eventually chased the British from their nest. Back at home things were considerably rougher. Little John foundered and failed. He didn't make it. He died just a fortnight after making his grand entrance.[11]

It was a time of mottled successes and small comforts.

As mentioned in chapter 6, in 1676 a Crown official visited Massachusetts and reported that the citizens "would make the world believe they are a free state." It took a century to live up to the reputation, but on 4 July 1776, Thomas Jefferson and the Continental Congress in Philadelphia declared the independence of the colonies, including the irascible Massachusetts. On 18 July the Declaration of Independence was read from the balcony of the Town House in Boston, after which every royal insignia in town was pried off wall and beam and burned in King Street.[12]

Would that winning independence were as easy as declaring it. Instead, Revere's military career devolved primarily into ill-suited bouts of timekeeping and babysitting. He was a man waiting for his war.

He had his moments. In the spring of 1777, Revere left Castle Island and traveled to Bridgewater, Massachusetts, where there were a furnace and a certain Frenchman, one Colonel Lewis Ansart, originally christened as the more flowery Louis de Maresquelle. Ansart was a foundryman, and Revere's job was to learn how to cast cannon, a job that suited his particular strengths nicely.[13]

But Paul spent most of his military service on Castle Island, dealing with ill-behaved soldiers who couldn't get enough provisions and had little to occupy them. There were several instances of deserters and drunkards in the ranks. The bottled-up nature of the service on the island also led to infighting, particularly with Captains William Todd and Winthrop Gray, both of whom filed a complaint against Revere. He answered it handily, but their resentment festered and would come back to later foul things for Paul.[14]

State service left Paul wanting. He wrote several patriot leaders about a position in the Continental army. He was refused on every attempt. The disappointment cut him right to the core. In April 1777 he wrote to his friend John Lamb, "I did expect before this to have been in the Continental Army, but do assure you, I have never been take notice off, by those whom I thought my friends, am obliged to be contented in this State's service."[15] Some months later, Sam Adams wrote Revere a condescending letter (basically confirming his complaint), saying that while "the Ambition of the Soldier is laudable . . . may it not be indulgd to Excess?" He said that he'd do everything he could do to get Paul a better post, but that he "should not lose the Sentiments of the Patriot" and serve where the "publick Good" was best served.[16] Paul was, of course, already doing so and

Engraving of Castle Island, on which Paul Revere spent much of his war. *Library of Congress.*

had been doing so and would continue doing so. He didn't need a big-brother reminder about something so basic—he wanted only the sympathy and help of a friend.

The war for Revere slogged on. In September 1777, Paul's regiment traveled on orders to Rhode Island, but after a brief campaign settled down for yet another winter at Castle Island. Then, in July 1778 it looked like there might be a worthy service. Revere's men, including Paul Jr., made their way again to Rhode Island. But the mission proved unimportant and useless.[17]

The weather was terrible, too rough for battle. He wrote to Rachel and was in surprisingly good spirits. You can tell from the text that he's spoiling for the fight; at the same time he's torn and wishes to be back with his wife and children:

> It is very irksome to be separated from *her* whom I so tenderly love, and from my little Lambs. It seems as if half Boston was here. I hope the affair will soon be settled. . . . I trust that Allwise being who has protected me will still protect me, and send me safely to the Arms of her whom it is my greatest happiness to call my own.[18]

Soon enough the campaign was over, and Revere was back in Boston.

As much as he loved and missed his family, Paul was anxious for glory, for a real fight. In 1779 it finally came.

Following the retreat of George Washington's army, the British commanded the ports of New York. They also commanded those of Nova Scotia, farther north. And smack-dab in between? Boston and a scattershot armada of American privateers whose only mission in life was to bedevil the king's ships, a task at which they excelled. So in June 1779, the British put a footprint in Penobscot Bay, Maine, a naval outpost where they could begin to repel the privateers and do damage to American shipping, as well as provide haven for nearby loyalists.

Jutting into Penobscot Bay was a triangular peninsula called Bagaduce, about a mile and three-quarters long. (Back then, the territory of Maine was part of the Massachusetts colony. And Bagaduce is today the town of Castine.) Some twenty miles inside the bay, it was the perfect place to erect a fort. Looking north, it was sheltered by a narrow harbor to the right. And to the left on western exposure several miles south of the gaping mouth of the Penobscot River, rugged slopes of some two hundred feet made landfall by enemy troops nearly impossible. It was only lightly populated then. Some barns and houses. Cornfields. Dense woodlands. By early July the Brits were settled in and starting to build a fort.[19]

But their efforts were no secret.

Authorities back in Boston got word about the Brits and began raising a massive force—an "expedition"—to roust the squatters. On 26 June Paul Revere received his orders:

Ordered—That Col°. Revere hold himself and one hundred of the Matrosses under his Command including proper Officers in readiness at one Hour's Notice to embark for the Defense of this State and to attack the Enemy at Penobscot.[20]

CHAPTER 20

Penobscot

*In which our hero finally finds his shining
moment to apply his martial skills to the
service and benefit of his country, only to
discover that fate steers both ships and men
in trajectories of tumult and tragedy for its
own grim and indiscernible pleasures.*

It wasn't easy or cheap, but the Bay Colony assembled a massive fleet. There were twenty-one sloops and schooners to transport men and eighteen armed vessels, including the *Warren*, the *Hazard*, and the aptly named *Tyrannicide*, thirty-nine ships in all. By Revere's counting, the armed ships sported 308 guns of various sizes, mostly 9-, 6-, and 4-pounders (cannons that shot iron balls of those weights). The *Warren*, commanded by the naval officer in charge of the ships and sailors, Commodore Dudley Saltonstall, had the biggest and most numerous guns, thirty-two 18- and 12-pounders.[1]

The land troops were commanded by Solomon Lovell, a wealthy farmer and local politician. Besides this current expedition, Revere and Lovell shared a previous excursion—to Fort William Henry during the French and Indian War. Both served at the same time under Colonel Richard Gridley. Back then Lovell was a first lieutenant; now he was a general. Twelve officers reported directly to him, including Paul, who headed up the artillery train. Much to his chagrin, another of his officers was Brigade Major William Todd, who'd filed bogus charges against Revere back on Castle Island. Revere made it clear that he would speak with Todd only in an official capacity.[2]

There was no hierarchy between Saltonstall and Lovell. Both possessed independent commands. They were to preserve and promote "the greatest harmony" with their counterpart so that "the Navy & Army may cooperate & assist each other." Their shared task was to "Captivate[,] Kill or Destroy the whole force of the Enemy there both by Sea & Land."[3]

Before departure Revere set about getting his guns in order. A committee was formed to determine how many he would need. It suggested ten in total—two 18-pounders, three 9-pounders, one 5.5-inch howitzer, and four brass 4-pounders. Paul didn't think this was enough firepower. He asked for six 18-pounders but didn't get them. He did make other adjustments. He subtracted one of the 9-pounders and added another howitzer.[4]

As mentioned, the pound designation had to do with the weight of round the cannon fired. An 18-pounder fired a solid iron ball of that weight. It could also fire grapeshot rounds—canvas sacks full of balls that scattered like shotgun pellets, only bigger. The weight of the cannon itself was another matter. Revere's 18-pounders weighed about four and a half thousand pounds apiece, and each required more than a dozen men to maneuver and operate. The benefit was that they were accurate at ranges slightly farther than a mile and could pummel enemy walls.[5] The smaller guns like the 4-pounders, were easier to manage on the battlefield. And the howitzer, while it had reduced range, fired at higher trajectories so it was more useful for lobbing bombs over walls into fortifications, rather than solid shot straight into the walls.[6] Revere knew that if they were taking a fort and other assorted armed batteries, he might need the upper hand that a howitzer provided.

By Monday, 19 July, the ships were under way, en route to Townshend (nowadays, Boothbay) to rendezvous with the assembled land troops, Massachusetts state militia from various Maine counties. The bobbing masts bristled the sky with bright ambitions, the billowing sails full of as much pride as wind. Unfortunately, as naval scholar George Buker notes, the fleet was not as formidable as it appeared. It was really "more akin to a naval gathering than a fleet," he says. "There was no time for fleet training." The assembled ships—a few state ships, a few Continental, the rest private—had different styles of operation and had never worked together before.[7] But they looked impressive.

The realities of their situation with the land troops were not so well camouflaged.

The flotilla arrived at Townshend two days later, the wind now out of their sails in more ways than one. The militia force, supposedly fifteen hundred strong, turned out to be just shy of nine hundred. And the assembly was a dispiriting bunch. After four years of fighting and funneling sons into the Continental army, the only men left were the dregs. One officer's appraisal: "Some sent Boys, old Men, and Invalids, if they belonged to the train Band, or Alarm List they were soldiers whether they could carry a Gun, walk a mile without crutches, or only Compos Mentis sufficient to keep themselves out of Fire & Water." Not too encouraging. Lovell inspected the men the following day, 22 July. A quarter "appear'd . . . unfit for the service."[8]

Revere was nonetheless lucky enough to find a 12-pound cannon in the militia's gear and added it to his own.[9]

After reviewing the men, Lovell called an evening meeting of his officers, along with Commodore Saltonstall and his officers. Penobscot was less than a day's journey. The initial fighting would begin very soon. Revere records, "There were some debates about the future operations of the Fleet, and the Army; nothing material was determined."[10] It would soon prove a pattern.

By the morning of Saturday, the twenty-fourth, the ragtag

army and undertrained navy were again under way. That evening they reached the mouth of Penobscot Bay in Maine and sent down anchors for the night.

The following morning Revere and the fleet traveled farther up the bay. As they drew closer, they could see what they were up against. Revere pulled out his telescope and spied the British encampments on the Bagaduce peninsula. "I could plainly see with my Glass, the enemy had begun a Fort, on one of the Heights."[11] Several batteries also stood with guns trained on the mouth of the harbor, and three British ships, the *Nautilus*, *Albany*, and *North*, waited on the eastern side of the peninsula at the harbor entrance, guarding the unfinished fort.

The Brits had their glasses out as well. On Saturday, they first caught sight of the massing enemy sails blowing inland like a menacing cloud bank. They scampered into defensive positions and readied for the storm.[12]

After some reconnoitering of the area and factoring the tricky winds and tides, Saltonstall ordered several of his ships into action. They swept in and fired on the trio at the harbor entrance while Lovell's men attempted a landing. But while the ships exchanged fire, Lovell could see that he was having trouble getting his men to shore and ordered them back. The Brits on shore took advantage, fired, and inflicted the first casualty of the expedition, one of the Americans' Indian allies onboard a landing vessel. On the morning of the twenty-sixth they tried it again and failed. They needed a new game plan.[13]

The war council met on the *Warren*. They decided to

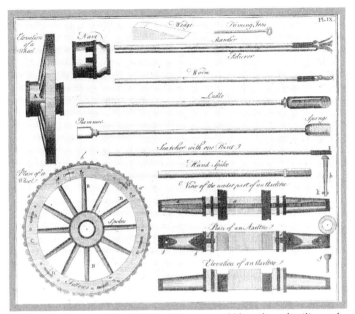

Artillery equipment with which Paul Revere would have been familiar and put to use in the Penobscot Expedition.
Library of Congress.

first take neighboring Bank's Island and a small British battery there. It was an ideal place to mount guns and fire upon the three British ships in the harbor and push them back up the harbor, which would make an easier job of landing the men on Bagaduce. They made their move. A detachment of marines, militia, and artillerymen landed and, with the help of one of Revere's fieldpieces, took the island.[14] Following action, Revere offloaded his two 18-pounders, his 12-pounder, and his second howitzer. Despite lousy weather, marines, sailors, and militiamen worked all night getting the fortifications in place. Revere's men positioned the cannons toward the British ships, and the next morning Revere and Lovell surveyed the positioning.[15]

By noon the two were back with the ships and agreed to meet with the other army and navy officers that night on the *Warren* to discuss invasion plans. With the battery in place at Bank's, the *Nautilus*, *Albany*, and *North* would be useless, which meant that the landing troops only had to worry about opposition from shore. Lovell had 850 men for the job. Revere put in his 80 artillerymen. Lovell ordered Revere to land with him, said Paul, "as a Corps de Reserve to the General, to leave my cannon, and take my muskets." The navy was in for 227 marines, giving a total landing force of 1,157 men. The action was planned for the twenty-eighth—just hours away.[16]

The invasion started in the cold foggy black of earliest morning. Marines and militia boarded their boats. Ships got into position. As the troops embarked, the *Tyrannicide*, *Hunter*, and *Sky Rocket* blasted through the trees at the top of the bluff, firing grapeshot and solid rounds in a thunderous barrage that lasted a full half hour.[17]

By then the marines landed at a point called Trask's Rock, musketfire from some three hundred Brits zinging by their shoulders and heads from above, plunking water, riveting boats, puncturing flesh. They gathered themselves against the foot of the precipice, scrounging whatever cover they could muster, and returned fire. The boats pushed off as soon as the men landed. Then, slinging their muskets over their shoulders and backs, they grabbed rocks, trees, saplings, and shrubs and dragged themselves up the steep incline, sliding and slipping backward, hauling and pulling forward. All the while British troops fired from above, and American soldiers below fired back to give cover.[18]

After the initial landing, Lovell came ashore, Revere and his men with him. As cannons boomed, muskets cracked, and men shouted orders, lead hailstones rained through the smoky clouds. They formed up and started up the two-hundred-foot cliff face.[19]

Over the top came the marines. The British manned a small battery with three cannons. Seeing the wave of Americans coming over the ridge, some of the men melted back. For those who remained, the marines made them wish they'd already begun the retreat. The gunfire intensified.[20]

Revere and the general crested the ridge, re-formed, and marched to the wooded area by the British line, where the fighting continued. The general called a halt. They could hear the gunfire through the trees, and then the jubilation. "[T]hey had got possession of the Heights," Paul said. The British scrambled back to their fort.[21] It was one of the most heroic and commendable actions fought in the war—followed shortly by several of the most disastrous and regrettable.

The Americans wasted no time reveling in their victory. Lovell ordered Revere to fetch the artillery from Bank's Island. "He desired me to be as expeditious as possible,"

Artillerists at work.
Library of Congress.

said Paul, "for he did not think it possible with what men he had, to storm the Enemy's forts." While he sent men to retrieve the cannons, he made preparations for the landing of the guns on Bagaduce. The following morning the operation was in full swing. Men brought the cannons down from Bank's, and on Bagaduce, Revere set carpenters to work hacking a road out of the brush so the guns could be hauled up to the summit and trained on the enemy fort.[22]

By midmorning Revere had spotted where he wanted the guns placed. He had a clear line to the enemy fort—what there was of it. He trained his telescope on the wall: "I could see that it was as high as a man's chin. . . ." Because they had no more time to build it higher, the British had begun to spike the ramparts to impede the Americans from storming over the top and impale the clumsy on their way. He could see that they had also built earthen mounds up to the edge from the inside, on which they'd mounted their cannons.[23]

As he was surveying the enemy, the smaller guns were landed, and then by afternoon one of the 18-pounders. Said Revere, "[T]hey were all hauled up near the lines." The next day they managed to get the other 18-pounder into place and let it rip. "[I]n the afternoon we opened the Battery and fired on the Enemy, with two 18 pounders, one twelve and a Howitzer." In Lovell's words, the cannons "play[ed] upon their grand Fort." The enemy blasted right back.[24]

The next day a deserter broke from the enemy and gave the story of the British force. "[T]hey were upwards of 900 strong," said Revere of the report; "they had 650 Soldiers, and near 300 Sailors." Lovell was convinced that he did not have enough men to take the fort. Revere thought otherwise. Given the number of transport ships, the Brits imagined the Americans had many more men than they did—perhaps more than double. Revere thought since the enemy didn't know how many men they had, they should storm: "[W]e being flushed with victory, I have no doubt they would have lain down their arms." Revere was right.

The British general later said that if the Americans had stormed the fort, he would have ordered just enough firing to allow his men to surrender without shame. Instead, Lovell sent to Boston for more men and ordered up the entrenching equipment. They settled down into a siege.[25]

Indecisive skirmishes, inconclusive jabber, and pointless action became the norm for the next week and a half. A British battery was taken, and then lost. A battery was erected to "annoy the Enemy's shipping" but placed too far away to do any good. War councils met to decide when and how to storm the fort, but nothing was decided. Lovell and Saltonstall went back and forth in a "you first"–"no, you first" exchange about who should attack what and when. Several looked at Saltonstall's refusal to enter the harbor and face the British ships as cowardice or maybe even collusion with the enemy. They called him "Sit-and-stall." But the problem was more complicated than wishing he'd simply sail in and blast the Brits to bits with his superior firepower. Maneuvering inside "that d—n hole," as he called the harbor, involved difficulties that the soldiers didn't understand; if he got inside and the wind changed, he'd be stranded at the mercy of the fort's guns and the enemy ships. His insistence that Lovell go in first was to keep his ships from sinking. But Lovell was in the same pickle. If he charged the land first, the British ships would blow his men to pieces on the shore. So who goes first?

The situation was like setting up a complicated series of moves in a chess game, and the impasse was so dispiriting and the time creeping by so noticeably that they even took a vote about ending the siege. Revere could see they were getting nowhere and voted to call it quits. Seven others did as well. While he was resolutely in favor of continuing the siege, Lovell's own diary betrays the sense that he might call the siege if he knew that enemy reinforcements were on their way. As it was, he held out hope that reinforcements of his own would arrive.[26]

Finally a solution. On Tuesday, 10 August, the land and sea forces reached agreement to attack simultaneously. The next day Lovell sent a large group of militiamen out on maneuvers beyond protection of the entrenchments, in his words, "to try my own men . . . how they wou'd act in a Body." It was a disaster. The Brits fired. The men panicked and beat a retreat so chaotic that Lovell became convinced that he couldn't live up to his agreement to storm the fort at the same time the ships attacked.[27]

The next morning, Thursday, 12 August, Revere accompanied Lovell to tell Saltonstall that Tuesday's agreement was off. The men weren't up to the job. Saltonstall was taken aback. Yet another council was called. Lovell ordered Revere to get the guns down from the batteries and move back to the transports.[28]

By early morning on Friday, 13 August (that couldn't bode well), Revere had the guns down to the beach, including both 18-pounders. Done with that, he attended the council. Another vote was taken on lifting the siege. The motion failed again, but two more agreed to end it. Revere's vote was unchanged. Nonetheless, they appeared to have decided on the original course, despite the circumstances. By late afternoon, Lovell rounded the rear of the fort with four hundred men, hiding under the cover of the bank, and got word to Saltonstall. Bring in the ships! But it was too late. Other ships were coming into view.[29]

"Our Ships get under sail," recorded Revere, "we supposing they were coming in, when to our great mortification, (the Fog clearing away) we see five sail of ships in the Bay." British reinforcements. It started to rain.[30]

Revere got his men and munitions to the transports that night. By morning the entire fleet was making good a retreat. Within hours they were dashing up the Penobscot River, away from the pursuing British ships. When Saltonstall's ships—and the cover they provided—passed the transport ships, the transports went to shore, where the men would at least be safe and not blown from the water. They offloaded what stores they could and torched the boats.

As the sun set, for miles up and down the river pandemonium reigned. Fires burned. Men shouted. Guns blasted. One small ship, unable to maneuver, drifted downriver toward the enemy fleet. On shore, Brigadier Peleg Wadsworth ordered Revere to send his barge after it. There is some confusion about how it transpired, but the short of it is that Paul refused because his chest was on board, "a small one which contained my Linen, some instruments and things of great Value to me; besides what little money I had with me." Though Revere eventually complied with the order, Wadsworth rebuked him and told him to expect arrest when he returned home. Not Paul's best moment. By then he was completely separated from his men. No wonder. Up and down the river, men melted into the woods.[31]

On the fifteenth, Paul reconnected with a handful of his men. Lovell was somewhere upriver, Wadsworth somewhere down. No way to get new orders, even if they felt they needed them at this point. They hoofed it into the brush. By the sixteenth, they made for the Kennebec River and then to Fort Western. Once there, several days later, Paul found most of his men. After supplying them the best he could, he ordered them back to Boston.[32]

A week later he was back in Boston, on 26 August, wearied, worn, and ready to put the whole disaster behind him. Wasn't to be. He returned to command at Castle Island. But things would not be the same. Some five hundred souls were lost or captured in the retreat. The entire navy was destroyed. The monetary cost alone staggered the state, more than £1.7 million. Someone would have to pay. The hunt for scapegoats began—perhaps not unexpected in the former land of the infamous witch trials. Commodore Saltonstall was first in mind. And then someone pointed a finger at Revere.

The charges came 6 September. Paul was relieved of his command and placed under house arrest, his military pay and rations frozen.

Captain Thomas J. Carnes leveled the accusations: that Paul was disobedient, neglectful of his duties, unsoldier-like, cowardly, and unconcerned for his men. Wadsworth jumped on board. And if the general outlandishness of the charges needed verification that a frame-up was under way, Paul's wartime nemesis Major Todd joined in as well. Someone was going under the oxcart wheels, and it wasn't going to be them.[33]

A committee was called to investigate and started hearing testimony on 22 September. Much to their chagrin, one witness after the other began to turn the tide against Todd and the others. It turned out that, barring a few cases, where they didn't get the facts wrong, they made them up entirely. Carnes, for instance, said that Revere didn't land with General Lovell on Bagaduce during the heat of battle. This was contradicted by Revere's own men—even Lovell himself.[34] But there was some wheat in all the tares. Revere had refused Wadsworth's order and had quit the field for home without orders from either Lovell or Wadsworth. How would he fare as the body weighed those charges?

It was early October before the committee came down with a verdict. They vindicated Lovell and Wadsworth and condemned Saltonstall (in absentia). And Revere? They were silent on his case. Revere was peeved. His military salary was on hold. His reputation and character were tarnished. And the committee didn't move to clear him or condemn him. Paul fired off a missive to the General Court to ask the committee to sit again.

They did and in mid-November finally rendered a verdict. They scuttled the more ridiculous charges and held him accountable for disputing Wadsworth's order and said that he was "not wholly justifiable" in returning to Boston without orders.

Revere thought he was still wronged and in January 1780 pushed for a proper court-martial. No go. He pushed again in March. A court-martial was granted but never called, and Paul was left hanging. While he'd finally been granted his back rations, Paul was maintaining a family of twelve in a depressed wartime economy with a sullied name. It was tough going. In May he moved his family out of the North End home and rented it out to make ends meet.[35]

In January 1781 he tried again, but got no action. Revere seems to have given up hope here. He quit requesting and got back to business.

In the meantime, the Revolution turned on its hinges in the Carolinas and Virginia. The British forces began suffering serious defeats, owing in large measure to discord between two royal commanders, General Henry Clinton in the North and General Charles Cornwallis in the South. With a timely arrangement between the French and Americans, Cornwallis met a match he could not best and was forced to surrender at Yorktown, effectively ending hostilities in the fall of 1781 and beginning the long process of negotiating the peace.

The war was over. The Americans had won.

Back in Boston, out of the blue, in February 1783 the court-martial met and reviewed Paul's case. Because Revere did, after rebuffing Wadsworth, eventually comply with his order, the court-martial acquitted him of this charge. And heading back to Boston without orders? The court-martial ruled that in such disarray, no proper or regular orders could have been given.

In short, Revere had done no wrong. He was vindicated.[36]

Todd and Carnes weren't happy with the verdict and dredged up all the old libels in newsprint salvos. These proved as ineffective as Saltonstall's exchanges at the mouth of Bagaduce Harbor. Revere fired back in a powerful, exhaustive response that took two issues of the paper to fit. Another shot came over Revere's bow. He fired back again. And that was the last word. He'd finally won the day and rescued his name.

Of course, with his finances in jeopardy, his family to secure, and his business to rebuild, Paul still had a lot left to prove. But energized by his victory and the newfound freedom of his country, Revere's creative output was about to explode in a rush of ingenuity and entrepreneurialism, while his social status and community responsibilities daily increased.

CHAPTER 21

Founding

*In which our hero, fresh from restoring
his good name, launches again into the
uncertain and choppy waters of commerce
and industry only to succeed in ways beyond
reckoning, establishing himself as one of
the new nation's first industrialists.*

It was easy to see that the teapots were different.

With tea embodying so much of the patriot struggle over taxation, regulation, and legislative nosiness, it's no surprise that the market for teapots dropped off after the Boston Tea Party. Revere doesn't seem to have even made any until almost a decade later when he crafted vessels in 1782 for cousin Thomas Hitchborn and Stephen and Isannah Bruce. By then the reason for abstaining was gone, and tea drinking came back in a big way. But unlike the bulbous designs he learned from his father, these teapots were squat cylinders with large wooden hoops for handles. He decorated with a delicate touch, characteristic of the neoclassical style. Already popular in Europe, this new approach, hearkening back to the simplicities and virtues of the Roman Republic, flowered in postwar America. Once again Revere was out in the lead with the new direction.[1] And teapots were only one sign. It was equally easy to see that most everything else was changing too.

The weariness that marked the Old World was replaced by a vivacity and spunk in the New that surpassed even its rowdy colonial days.[2] Revere took that new energy and released it in a surge of creativity and invention, developing, adopting, and adapting new technologies; embarking on new trades and new ventures; grabbing every lever, using every edge, maneuvering every advantage he could find or make to expand his business, better his station, and improve his family's lot. One overview example: Revere's shop years are divided into two periods, 1761–75 and 1779–97. Just looking at silver objects like flatware, tea and coffee sets, and personal items such as buckles, buttons, and thimbles, in the first period his output was significant, some 1,145 total items. But in the second, Revere's output of the same jumped 368 percent—4,210 such objects.[3] Always inquisitive, his relentless experimentation and nimble applications allowed him to constantly do more.

Not all of his ventures were profitable. In 1782, for instance, he signed on to a partnership with a man to make clock jacks. Three years later, Revere pulled out, worse for the deal.[4]

Then in 1783 he tried something new. He handed over day-to-day management of the silver shop to Paul Jr. and opened a store that sold wares from the shop and items imported from England, such as paper, pencils, sealing wax, fabric, and hosiery. He found trouble in the financing department, however. He couldn't get enough credit from British merchants and had his own cash tied up in U.S. government securities. It turned out to be more headache than he desired, but he kept at it.[5]

Not that he relied on it. Revere was always straddling more than one horse. While the store failed to garner the returns he desired, he experimented with sheet silver. Using a plating mill, he could flatten silver with greater uniformity and speed than by beating it flat with hammers in the traditional method. The trick was getting one. It was illegal to ship tools from England, even after the peace Treaty of Paris. Wrote one of his suppliers back in Britain, "It is with Difficulty we are able to get any tools shipt as they fall under the Denomination of prohibhitted wares[;] you will oblige me by keeping it unknown to the Captain who conveys them as my future conveniency in shipping may be hurt."[6] Paul was a New Englander, right? He smuggled it. Despite the restrictions, in 1785 he bought his mill and began perfecting its use and reaping the reward of the uptick in productivity.[7]

Not only could a plating mill flatten metal, but it could fuse sheets together—doing as its name suggested, plating one metal on the other. Revere had another method for plating as well, and between the two in the 1780s cranked

Paul Revere with his wars behind him
and his future ahead.
Library of Congress.

out a dizzying number of plated objects.[8] What's more, he experimented with new designs, constantly adjusting style and technique to match or anticipate customer demand. He even traded a bit on his reputation as a horseman by crafting solid silver and plated tack and gear like stirrups and bridle buckles.[9]

All this while the Massachusetts economy was in a slump. Exports were a quarter in 1786 of what they'd been in 1774, but that didn't stop Revere.[10]

As his financial situation improved, so did the lot of his children. His older children, like daughters Deborah and Frances and son Paul Jr., all married in the 1780s and gave Paul and Rachel a string of grandchildren in quick succession. And Paul and Rachel were far from finished; they had five more children in the same period. The younger children did not receive the same writing school education their father did; they were sent to Latin schools, just as Paul's "betters" were when he was a boy. And Paul, son of a French refugee, was later able to send Joseph Warren (named for his dearly departed friend) and John abroad to study.

Revere's civic role enlarged along with his commercial one. In at least one very singular instance, both his civic and his commercial roles came together.

Since independence the United States operated under the Articles of Confederation. That changed in 1787 when delegates in Philadelphia drafted and adopted the Constitution. Before it could go into effect, however, it had to be ratified by different states—a long and noisy process. Several states had already signed on, but Massachusetts remained undecided. More than undecided, the delegates were split just about down the middle; some for, some against. By early 1788, Revere and a group of artisans weighed in. They met at the Green Dragon and worked up some resolutions. If the Constitution were adopted, "trade and navigation would revive and increase, and employ and subsistence afforded to many of their townsmen, then suffering for the want of the necessaries of life" went one resolution. But, went another, if the new charter floundered, then "the small remains of commerce yet left would be annihilated; the various trades and handicrafts dependent thereon decay; the poor be increased, and many worthy and skilful mechanics compelled to seek employ and subsistence in strange lands."[11]

Revere took the resolutions straight to his old friend Samuel Adams, one of the few delegates who could tip the whole convention. The trouble was that he seemed to be on the fence. Paul gave him a push. He told Adams that the artisans had met at the Green Dragon and drafted the resolutions.

"How many mechanics were at the Green Dragon when these resolutions were passed?"

"More, sir, than the Green Dragon could hold," Paul answered.

"And where were the rest, Mr. Revere?"

"In the streets, sir."

"And how many were in the streets?"

"More, sir, than there are stars in the sky."[12]

Revere was in the Federalist camp, which favored a more vigorous central government than did the anti-Federalists, the Republicans. A major reason expressed here was clearly about the freedom and advantages to trade that the Constitution would afford. In the end, Adams concurred with his old friend, and Massachusetts signed on to the Constitution.

That same year, Paul became a founder of a different sort. He opened Boston's first bronze and iron foundry in North Boston and started pumping out hammers, anvils, nails, spikes, bolts, and other hardware, even cannons, which he had learned about casting during the war. He inquired of other established founders and read a good deal to acquire the knowledge necessary to create a quality product. Soon he set his ambitions on a real challenge.

Lost in all the news of the Boston Massacre was this notice in the 12 March 1770 *Boston Gazette*: "A Bell Foundry lately erected by Aaron Hobart of Abington (By an air furnace) where bells are cast of any size suitable for Churches, equal to and cheaper than can be imported."[13] Hardly any bells were forged in America before Hobart's foundry (the Liberty Bell is a notable exception), and relatively few afterward. Paul saw an opening. When Hobart decided to close up shop, he helped Paul get started in the business. And Paul's first customer? His childhood church, the Cockerel, which in 1792 needed a new chime.

Bell casting is notoriously tough. Everything affects the final sound: the size, the shape, the combination of copper, tin, zinc, lead, and silver in the casting, even the source metals matter, as one writer notes, "for the metals of different mines differ as to the sonorous properties as well as in brittleness." The same writer goes on to list several other complicating factors, all of which work to excuse Paul the faults of his first effort, which turns out to have been "harsh, panny, and unmusical." The church was still happy to hang the 911-pounder and let it ring. It was the first bell cast in Boston. There would be many more; between 1792 and 1828, Revere and Son (as the business was called when he brought in Joseph Warren) cast 398 bells for churches, ships, plantations, and more. It's no stretch to say that Revere's bells were heard around the world.[14]

His timing couldn't have been better. It took about twenty years for postwar trade (and with it the ship-building industry) to really rebound. In the 1780s European-made ships crowded American wharves, but the tide turned by the end of the century. One Massachusetts shipyard between 1799 and 1801 averaged twenty-three new ships a year.[15] Paul's foundry was able to outfit ships galore with all manner of iron, brass, and copper fittings.

In the realm of copper he was becoming particularly expert, surpassing any other tradesman in New England. He'd perfected a unique method of melting the metal and drawing the malleable strands into spikes. It was something thought impossible. Just the kind of job for Revere: "I . . . found that it was a Secret, that lay in very few Breasts in England. I determined if possible to find the Secret & have the pleasure to say, that after a great many trials and considerable expense I gained it."[16] The skill would soon pay off.

Boston's population shot up in the decade following the war. The population at the end of the conflict was about twelve thousand. In seven years it had shot up to eighteen thousand. One of the concerns of a burgeoning population was a proper police force. In 1791 the town called a committee to work on a solution. On the committee, along with leading lights like future president John Quincy Adams, Charles Bulfinch, Thomas Dawes Jr., and William Tudor, served Paul Revere.[17]

Paul's persistence in the Masons continued, serving as grand master of the Grand Lodge of Massachusetts for several years in the middle 1790s. But the capstone to Paul's

Masonic life came in the form of a cornerstone. On 4 July 1795, the cornerstone of a new State House was laid, and the government asked that the Masons finally get down to some real masonry. There was a grand parade and grand orations. After the stone had been properly set in place, Paul Revere spoke:

> Worshipfull Brethren. I congratulate you on this auspicious day:—When the Arts and Sciences are establishing themselves in our happy country, a Country distinguished from the rest of the World, by being a Government of Laws, where Liberty has found a safe and secure abode, and where her sons are determined to support and protect her. . . . May we, my Brethren, so square our actions thro life as to show to the World of Mankind, that we mean to live within the compass of Good Citizens, that we wish to stand upon a level with them, that when we part we may be admitted into the Temple where Reigns Silence and Peace.[18]

That same year, he worked with other leading artisans to update the apprenticeship laws and form an association of mechanics. Several meetings and deliberations were called, and when it was complete, Revere announced, "The Constitution of the Associated Mechanics of the Town of Boston will be ready for signing on Saturday next, at Mr. Ebenezer Larkin's Bookstore in Cornhill." Paul's was the first of eighty-three signatures applied to the document. Paul Jr. signed on too. In a meeting called for 16

April—almost twenty years to the day after his famous ride—the artisans elected officers and chose Paul as the president of the group.[19] He was also a principal mover in the incorporation of the Massachusetts Mutual Fire Insurance Company.[20]

Revere found other civic and community roles to fill, even some that don't seem too likely. In 1796, for instance, he took the office of county coroner. Over the next five years he conducted some forty-six inquests; he charged $119.11 for the first five.[21]

He desired other sorts of public service, particularly at the federal level. He inquired about positions at the National Mint and the Excise Office, but didn't get the jobs. Still, it turned out the best way he could serve his country was through commerce.

Along with cannon for the state of Massachusetts, he started casting cannon for the American military in 1794. He worked through his old Boston contact Henry Knox, who now headed up the United States War Department. The order was for ten howitzers.[22] His performance got him future ordnance work, but the real excitement— typical for Boston—was at the water's edge.

Paul got wind that the United States frigate *Constitution* would be built in Boston, in the North End near his foundry. He fired off a letter to the government, saying that he could supply bolts, braces, and similar items, "as cheap as any one, and as well." He got the job.[23] And others too, including the frigate *Essex*. Applying for that job in 1798 to the new naval secretary, Benjamin Stoddard, Revere suggested that if he could get enough raw materials, "I would undertake to roll Sheet Copper for Sheathing Ships, &c."[24]

Revere started working with copper when he was a young man, primarily engraving copperplate for printing. Later he'd developed unique forging methods for bolts and nails. But all of his experience was with copper that had already been refined. Now he was getting into something truly monumental—smelting ore (which was notoriously hard to come by), refining the metal (which took several challenging steps), and rolling it in sheets (which required specialized equipment to accomplish well).

With the success of his business ventures, in 1800 Revere finally bought another house. It was on Charter Street near his foundry, where he could be close to work and bring his work home. He had a yard behind the house where he would display and test his bells. Local boys would congregate as the chimes were struck with a hammer to hear them sound. Once a group got a little too close. "Take care, boys!" he said as he drew them back with his walking stick. "If that hammer should hit your head, you'd ring louder than those bells do."[25]

Paul's most important purchase that year was not, however, in Boston. It was in the countryside of Canton Dale. He was now sixty-five years old. Most men his age were dead, not expanding businesses. But that's what he did.

In January 1800 he selected a site with a river running through it to erect a copper mill. Then in March he wrote his congressman, Harrison Gray Otis, and made an offer: "[I]f the government would send me a quantity [of ore for smelting] and pay my expenses I would make furnaces and make myself"—the fact that he'd never smelt an ounce of copper ore didn't give Revere a moment's pause—"master of this business."[26]

Although the U.S. government had been previously burned by two failed copper refiners, Revere's letter had the desired effect. The benefits of sheathing ship bottoms in copper were worth the risk, and Revere had the kind of reputation that made him a good bet. The government asked him to come to Philadelphia in May, from which he left with a contract and a promise for a barrel of ore to get started. His first efforts were less than impressive, for which he apologized in a letter to the secretary, but nonetheless, he'd done it. To really do a good job, however, he'd need a loan to buy proper equipment; he'd pay it back in copper sheets.[27]

It was rough going at first, because with Thomas Jefferson's new presidential administration coming into power in 1801, Paul found it tough to get paid—just one of many reasons for which Federalist Paul Revere found frustration in the new Republican administration. He finally got the promised loan of $10,000 in the summer of '01. He paid it off in less than a year. In the meantime, Paul also sheathed the dome of the Massachusetts State House with almost 8,500 pounds of copper.

By 1802 his factory was cranking up for mass production. He employed five men. Within a few years the payroll would grow to twelve workers. After a bumper year in 1803, the only significant drop in revenues came in 1807, caused by a trade war with France and England. America's response, the Embargo Act, just worsened matters. Shipping suffered first; everything else followed. Bankruptcies blossomed, and weeds grew up around the unused docks in Boston.[28] "The miserable conduct of our Rulers in laying that cursed Embargo," wrote Revere, "had nearly deprived us of selling copper for ships."[29]

It was an old story that was told time and again in Paul's life: there is no greater destroyer of wealth than misguided government. The only antidote short of revolution was vigorous political activism and even more vigorous entrepreneurial effort. Paul was handy at both, but now in his old age his strength lay more in the latter.

By 1811, despite the embargo, his company was worth $50,000—a staggering amount for the time—and his factory produced several tons of copper a week. The output helped other innovators get their dreams off the drawing board and into action. Some of Revere's copper, for instance, went to a man named Robert Fulton, who was busy perfecting the steam engine and needed thick sheets of copper for his experimental boilers.[30]

CHAPTER 22

Departures

In which our hero is laid to rest in hope
of the resurrection, saying before his death,
"In my last Stage, how blest am I . . ."
and loved and admired by many after his passing.

In 1811, at age seventy-six, Paul Revere finally retired from business and handed the reins to his son Joseph Warren Revere.

Just before, he penned a lengthy poem about the joys of living at his summer home in Canton Dale. He paints the very picture of tranquillity and mild country joys. He talks about his dear Rachel, "My Better Half . . . lolling in her chair." He mentions listening to the robins and the wrens that live nearby, sitting under an oak and reading, or taking his "Dog and Gun" out for the day. He mentions going to visit friends with Rachel,

To walk thro Groves, and grass'y Fields
Contemplating what Nature yealds.[1]

Sometimes she yielded unwelcome news. The healthy Revere lived a long and vigorous life, but the deaths of many of his friends and family punctuated the blessing. He outlived more than a few, not just brave young Joseph Warren, cut down so early. Sam Adams died in 1803. John Hancock passed a decade before in 1793 and James Otis ten years before that, in 1783 (struck incidentally by lightning, which he eerily foretold). An ocean away Thomas Hutchinson preceded his old rival Otis into heaven's bosom by three years. And there were countless others. Fellow silversmiths Samuel Minott and Benjamin Burt, for instance, passed away in 1803 and 1805, respectively.

Sarah bore him eight children, Rachel the same. Paul outlived most of his "little lambs." The only daughter of Sarah's to outlive him was Mary. Four of Rachel's children lived beyond their parents—Harriet, Maria, John, and Joseph Warren, the last of whom lived to be ninety-one. Not even Paul's oldest boy, Paul Jr., made it beyond. The boy who cared for the family when dad was out on express rides, who guarded the house during the British occupation, who served in the Massachusetts militia with his father, who ran and operated the family silversmith shop, died of tuberculosis in January 1813.

Then the greatest pain of all: the gentle and capable Rachel Revere, Paul's constant companion, succumbed to a brief but powerful illness and closed her eyes for the last time 26 June 1813. She was sixty-eight. Paul had her borne to the Granary burial yard, where so many of the family already rested.

There was hope in grief. Even if they couldn't have quoted it word for word, both Paul's Puritan and Huguenot forebears believed Calvin's observation that "he alone has made solid progress in the gospel who has acquired the habit of meditating continually on a blessed resurrection."[2] Paul, eyes down to the fresh soil over Rachel's grave, could, in the words of Esther Forbes, "look forward resolutely to the day of doom when the last trump would sound—and what a flight of Hitchbourns and Reveres would rise up about him!—all saved, no longer to fight the weakness of their flesh, but radiant with their immortality."[3] He would see all his family again. And especially Rachel, dear Rachel.

For now he remained active, riding his horses and staying versed in political debates of the day. In 1814 he even volunteered to help defend Boston from the Brits yet again as the unpopular War of 1812 threatened his home.[4] The eighty-year-old Revere circulated a petition, primarily among his beloved North End mechanics "for the Defence of the Town and Naval Arsenal," offering "our services to His Excellency the Commander-in-Chief, to be directed in such manner as he shall consider at this eventful crisis most conducive to the Public Good."[5] The government was all for it, and the mechanics helped build Fort Strong to aid in the protection of their town.

He finally settled down in 1816 and penned his will. "In

the name of God, Amen," he wrote, "I, Paul Revere . . . Esquire, being in good health and of sound memory, but knowing that all men must die do make and declare this to be my last will and testament." He made arrangements for his children, for his grandchildren, cousins, and others, seeing to all their needs with all he had.[6]

And then he died.

It was 10 May 1818. He was eighty-three and passed from his house on Charter Street in Boston to that "Temple where Reigns Silence and Peace." But there was little silence in Boston. It was a Sunday, and overhead rang bell after bell that he had cast.[7]

The newspapermen were quick to their pens. "During his protracted life, his activity in business and benevolence, the vigor of his mind, and the strength of his constitution were unabated," ran one of many notices. "Seldom has the tomb closed upon a life so honorable and useful."[8]

Revere's Family

Paul Revere (1734–1818) had a remarkably long life; he lived to be 83 years old. His father, Apollos (1702–1754), died young by comparison, just 51. Paul's mother, Deborah (1704–1777), lived to be 73.

Paul outlived all his siblings, and there were a lot of them. Apollos and Deborah had some eleven children. The first I did not mention in the narrative, John (1730), was born seven months after their marriage but died within a year. Several of the children died in infancy. Paul's younger brother, Thomas, died at war during the Revolution. Three—John, the tailor (1741–1808), and his littlest sisters, Mary (1743–1801) and Elizabeth (1745–1811)—lived to see the nineteenth century, but most died long before.

In 1757, Paul married Sarah Orne (1736–1773). The couple had eight children in all:

1. Deborah (1758–1797)
2. Paul (1760–1813)

3. Sarah (1762–1791)

4. Mary (1764–1765)

5. Frances (1766–1799)

6. Mary (1768–1853)

7. Elizabeth (1770–1805)

8. Isanna (1772–1773)

I think biographer Esther Forbes was first to notice that Paul and Sarah were remarkably regular; all eight children were born on even-numbered years, two years apart. The infant mortality was thankfully lessened from the previous generation, but many of Paul and Sarah's children still lived short lives; only Mary outlived her father.

Sarah died in 1773, and the house was then in sore need of a mother's care, as one family member put it. That same year Paul married Rachel Walker (1745–1813). They had eight more children:

1. Joshua (1774–1801)

2. John (1776, birth and death in same year)

3. Joseph Warren (1777–1868)

4. Lucy (1780, birth and death in same year)

5. Harriet (1782–1860)

6. John (1783–1786)

7. Maria (1785–1847)

8. John (1787–1847)

The last five get short shrift in the narrative. I merely mention Paul's rapidly accumulating grandchildren and then say that Paul and Rachel were themselves not finished. The five children came in quick succession, all between 1780 and 1787. Rachel was then in her late thirties and early forties, Paul in his late forties and early fifties.

Rachel's children lived much longer lives than those of Sarah's, particularly Joseph Warren, who lived all the way through the Civil War, dying in 1868. (Something about that number, by the way, Joseph Warren had eight children as well.) Joseph Warren, as it happened, took over the family business from his father.

It is interesting to consider Apollos sailing to America as a refugee, impoverished, indentured, with little in his future except the hope of religious freedom and learning a trade in America. Then think of his grandson, John Revere, part of a large and established family, leaving America's shores to study in Europe and returning to the United States to become a professor of medicine. Or John's sister Maria, whose travels were even more exotic; after marrying Joseph Balestier, a planter and the first U.S. consul to the Far East, she set sail for Singapore in 1834 where she lived the rest of her life.

The weariness of the old was traded for the vibrancy of the new.

Sources: Donald M. Nielsen, "The Revere Family," *New England Historical and Genealogical Register* 145 (1991). Patrick M. Leehey, "Reconstructing Paul Revere," in *Paul Revere: Artisan, Businessman, and Patriot* (Boston: Paul Revere Memorial Association, 1988). Esther Forbes, *Paul Revere and the World He Lived In* (Boston: Houghton Mifflin, 1942), 56, 473–478. Also see: Valentine Mott, *A Biographical Memoir of the Late John Revere, M.D.* (New York: Joseph H. Jennings, 1847).

Notes

Epigraphs

1. J. Hector St. John de Crèvecoeur, *Letters from an American Farmer and Sketches of 18th Century America,* ed. Albert E. Stone (New York: Penguin, 1981), 69.
2. Stephen L. Longenecker, *Shenandoah Religion, 1716–1865* (Waco: Baylor University Press, 2002), 48.

Prologue

1. All events and quoted material taken from Paul Revere, *Paul Revere's Three Accounts of His Famous Ride,* 4th ed. (Boston: Massachusetts Historical Society, 2000), third account. The full account of Paul Revere's famous ride is covered in chapter 17.

1. Arrivals

1. Edmund Morgan, *The Puritan Dilemma* (Boston: Little, Brown, 1958), 39.
2. Ibid., 9.
3. Josiah Quincy, *A Municipal History of the Town and City of Boston* (Boston: Little, Brown, 1852), 2, 328. The American Indians called the peninsula *Shawmut.* As a name,

Trimountain didn't last long. Settlers tagged the town Boston shortly after putting down roots.

4. Morgan, *Dilemma*, 55–59. Samuel Eliot Morison, *Builders of the Bay Colony* (Boston: Houghton Mifflin, 1958), 77–80.

5. See, e.g., Francis Bacon's essay "On Plantations," in Francis Bacon, *Bacon's Essays*, ed. Guy Montgomery (New York: Macmillan, 1930), 86–88.

6. Morison, *Builders*, 25. See also Robert Shackleton, *The Book of Boston* (Philadelphia: Penn Publishing, 1920), 70–71.

7. John C. Miller, *Origins of the American Revolution* (Boston: Little, Brown, 1943), 11.

8. Mark Kurlansky, *Cod* (New York: Penguin, 1997), 70–74.

9. Elbridge Henry Goss, *The Life of Colonel Paul Revere*, vol. 1 (Boston: Joseph George Cupples, 1891), 3–8. Patrick M. Leehey, "Reconstructing Paul Revere," in *Paul Revere: Artisan, Businessman, and Patriot* (Boston: Paul Revere Memorial Association, 1988), 18–20. The case of Protestant Huguenots having to practice their religion on the sly mirrors that of the Catholic recusants in Anglican Britain.

10. Esther Forbes, *Paul Revere and the World He Lived In* (Boston: Houghton Mifflin, 1942), 6, 49. G. B. Warden, *Boston, 1689–1776* (Boston: Little, Brown, 1970), 25–26.

2. ASCENT

1. Edmund S. Morgan, *The Puritan Family* (New York: Harper, 1966), 120–21. Robert Francis Seybolt, *Apprenticeship and Apprenticeship Education in Colonial New England and New York* (New York: Arno, 1969), 29.

2. Goss, *Life of Colonel Paul Revere*, 1:10. Leehey, "Reconstructing Paul Revere," 20–21. Getting one's name changed wasn't a formal affair. Even in official town documents, such as the minutes of the town selectmen meetings, Paul Revere's name is variously spelled Revere, Reviere, Reveire, and Reverie a full generation after his dad had changed it.

3. David Hackett Fischer, *Paul Revere's Ride* (New York: Oxford University Press, 1994), 6.

4. Leehey, "Reconstructing Paul Revere," 20.

5. Perry Miller, ed., *The American Puritans* (New York: Columbia University Press, 1956), 171.

6. Alonzo Lewis and James R. Newhall, *History of Lynn, Essex County, Massachusetts* (Boston: John L. Shorey, 1865), 119, 137–38, 142, 204–5, 221. James R. Newhall, *Ye Great and General Courte in Collonie Times* (Lynn, MA: Nichols Press, 1897), 290. May Alden Ward, *Old Colony Days* (Boston: Roberts Brothers, 1897), 101.

7. Donald M. Nielsen, "The Revere Family," *New England Historical and Genealogical Register* 145 (1991): 292–93.

8. Goss, *Life of Colonel Paul Revere*, 1:11–12. Nielsen, "Revere Family," 293.

9. Bernard Bailyn, *The Ordeal of Thomas Hutchinson* (Cambridge: Harvard University Press, 1974), 10.

10. The Cockerel's weather vane was the handiwork of coppersmith and church deacon Shem Drowne. His artful weather vanes adorned the finest buildings in Boston: a glass-eyed grasshopper atop Faneuil Hall, an Indian with bow and arrow on Province House, and an arrangement of hollow balls and a five-pointed star on the Old North Church. The last building, also called Christ Church, was the church from which two lights shone in the spire on the night of Paul Revere's famous ride.

11. Warden, *Boston*, 102–3. Warden pins the second smallpox outbreak in 1730, though most cite 1729.

12. Ibid., 103.

13. David Hume, *An Enquiry Concerning Human Understanding and Other Essays*, ed. Ernest C. Mossner (New York: Washington Square, 1963), 267.

14. Nielsen, "Revere Family," 293. Fischer, *Paul Revere's Ride*, 6, 374n4.

15. Harlow Giles Unger, *John Hancock* (New York: Wiley, 2000), 30–31.

16. John K. Alexander, *Samuel Adams* (Lanham: Rowman and Littlefield, 2002), 5.

17. Ibid., 4–7.

3. MOXIE

1. Jayne E. Triber, *A True Republican* (Amherst: University of Massachusetts Press, 1998), 7.
2. Goss, *Life of Colonel Paul Revere*, 1:76, 79. Clarence S. Brigham, *Paul Revere's Engravings*, 2nd ed. (New York: Atheneum, 1969), 13–15. Forbes, *Paul Revere and the World*, 29.
3. Morgan, *Family*, 87–88.
4. Quincy, *Municipal History*, 9.
5. Morgan, *Family*, 98–100. Also see Paul Leicester Ford, *The New-England Primer* (New York: Dodd, Mead, 1897), 277–81. Ford's book covers the origin and development of the primer.
6. Ford, *New-England Primer*, 328.
7. Henry Hawley, "Rococo Silver in Europe," *Magazine Antiques*, January 1995.
8. Text of the agreement can be found in several places, including Forbes, *Paul Revere and the World*, 31–32, and Mary Kent Davey Babcock, *Christ Church, Salem Street, Boston* (Boston: Thomas Todd, 1947), 192–93. I transcribed the version here from David Hackett Fischer's facsimile reprinted in *Paul Revere's Ride*, 13.
9. Fischer, *Paul Revere's Ride*, 12.
10. Alden Bradford, *Memoir of the Life and Writings of Rev. Jonathan Mayhew* (Boston: C. C. Little & Co., 1838), 28–29.
11. Perry Miller, ed., *The American Puritans* (New York: Columbia University Press, 1982), 138. While it is impossible to nail the dates of Paul's attendance, he might well have heard this sermon, preached 30 January 1750. For lengthy discussion of this sermon, see chapter 6 of Charles W. Akers, *Called unto Liberty* (Cambridge: Harvard University Press, 1964), 81–97.
12. For instance, Huguenots like François Hotman, Theodore Beza, and Philippe du Plessis-Mornay; and Puritans like John Ponet, George Buchanan, and Samuel Rutherford. Later writers like John Milton and John Locke took up where these men left off. See Julian H. Franklin, ed.,

trans., *Constitutionalism and Resistance in the Sixteenth Century* (New York: Pegasus, 1969); Douglas F. Kelly, *The Emergence of Liberty in the Modern World* (Phillipsburg, NJ: Presbyterian and Reformed, 1992); and J. N. Figgis, *Political Thought from Gerson to Grotius: 1414–1625* (New York: Harper, 1960).

13. See Alice Baldwin, *The New England Clergy and the American Revolution* (New York: Frederick Ungar, 1965). As President John Adams later said, "The original plantation of our country was occasioned, her continual growth has been promoted, and her present liberties have been established by these generous theories." John Adams, *The Works of John Adams*, vol. 6, ed. Charles Francis Adams (Boston: Little, Brown, 1851), 3.

14. Bradford, *Rev. Jonathan Mayhew*, 465–70. Akers, *Called unto Liberty*, 113–32.

15. Goss, *Life of Colonel Paul Revere*, 1:17–18.

16. Forbes, *Paul Revere and the World*, 454.

4. Foes

1. Quincy, *Municipal History*, 5.
2. Triber, *True Republican*, 21. Forbes, *Paul Revere and the World*, 40, 106. Goss, *Life of Colonel Paul Revere*, 1:105–6.
3. Warden, *Boston*, 142–44.
4. Ibid., 144.
5. Isaiah Thomas, *The History of Printing in America*, 2nd ed., vol. 2 (New York: Burt Franklin, 1874), 521.
6. Baldwin, *New England Clergy*, 85.
7. Peter Orlando Hutchinson, *The Diary and Letters of His Excellency Thomas Hutchinson, Esq.*, vol. 1 (New York: Burt Franklin, 1971), 7–8.
8. Fred Anderson, *The War That Made America* (New York: Viking, 2005), 55–63.
9. Goss, *Life of Colonel Paul Revere*, 1:19–22.
10. Forbes, *Paul Revere and the World*, 44.
11. Francis Parkman, *Montcalm and Wolfe* (New York: Barnes and Noble, 2005), 207.

12. Ibid., 207–8.

13. Ibid., 215–16.

14. Ibid., 209.

15. Ibid.

16. Another of the men serving with Paul that summer was a wealthy young farmer, Solomon Lovell, who would later become a general in the Massachusetts militia and would play a part with Revere in the disastrous Penobscot Expedition (about which, see chapter 20).

17. Forbes, *Paul Revere and the World*, 56. Nielsen, "Revere Family," 296, 298.

18. Anderson, *War That Made America*, 111–12.

19. David A. Copeland, "Fighting for a Continent," *Early America Review*, Spring 1997, http://www.earlyamerica.com/review/spring97/newspapers.html.

20. Ibid.

21. Ibid.

22. Ibid.

5. FRIENDS

1. David R. Brigham, "Paul Revere Silver at the Worcester Art Museum," *Magazine Antiques*, April 2000.

2. Janine E. Skerry, "The Revolutionary Revere," in *Paul Revere: Artisan, Businessman, and Patriot* (Boston: Paul Revere Memorial Association, 1988), 48–49. Kathryn C. Buhler, *Paul Revere, Goldsmith* (Boston: Museum of Fine Arts, n.d.), item 13.

3. Nielsen, "Revere Family," 293, 299.

4. Forbes, *Paul Revere and the World*, 77.

5. Bruce C. Daniels, *Puritans at Play* (New York: St. Martin's Griffin, 1996), 145, 147.

6. Edith J. Steblecki, *Paul Revere and Freemasonry* (Boston: Paul Revere Memorial Association, 1985), 3.

7. David Barton, *The Question of Freemasonry and the Founding Fathers* (Aledo: WallBuilders, 2005), 37–47. S. Brent Morris, "The Post Boy Sham Exposure of 1723," in *Freemasonry in Context*, ed. Arturo de Hoyos and S. Brent Morris (Lanham: Lexington Books, 2004), 130.

8. Steblecki, *Paul Revere and Freemasonry*, 18.

9. John Cary, *Joseph Warren* (Urbana: University of Illinois Press, 1961), 17–18.

10. Steblecki, *Paul Revere and Freemasonry*, 11.

11. Elbridge Henry Goss, *The Life of Colonel Paul Revere*, vol. 2 (Boston: Howard W. Spurr, 1898), 667.

12. Forbes, *Paul Revere and the World*, 66.

13. Goss, *Life of Colonel Paul Revere*, 2:667–68. Forbes, *Paul Revere and the World*, 66–67. Triber, *True Republican*, 36.

6. Grudges

1. John Adams, *The Legal Papers of John Adams*, vol. 2, ed. L. Kinvin Wroth and Hiller B. Zobel (Cambridge: Belknap, 1965), 98–101.

2. Miller, *Origins of the American Revolution*, 7.

3. Adam Smith, *The Wealth of Nations* (New York: Modern Library, 1994), 970.

4. Arthur D. Pierce, *Smugglers' Woods* (New Brunswick: Rutgers University Press, 1960), 8.

5. Charles Adams, *For Good and Evil* (Lanham: Madison, 1994), 264–65.

6. Regarding the creation and controversy of writs of assistance in general, see John Adams, *Legal Papers*, 2:106–47, as well as Josiah Quincy, *Reports of Cases Argued and Adjudged in the Superior Court of Judicature of the Province of Massachusetts Bay Between 1761 and 1772* (Boston: Little, Brown, 1865), 395–540.

7. Charles Adams, *For Good and Evil*, 258, 261.

8. England's Navigation Acts provoked three separate wars with the Dutch. J. A. Williamson, *Great Britain and the Empire* (London: Adam and Charles Black, 1946), 37.

9. Melvyn Bragg, *The Adventure of English* (New York: Arcade, 2003), 111.

10. Benjamin Woods Labaree, *The Boston Tea Party* (Boston: Northeastern University Press, 1979), 6–10.

11. Mark A. Noll, *The Rise of Evangelicalism* (Downers Grove: IVP, 2003), 14.

12. Thomas Hutchinson, *The Hutchinson Papers*, vol. 2 (Albany: Prince Society, 1865), 232.

13. Hiller B. Zobel, *The Boston Massacre* (New York: Norton, 1971), 15.

14. Edmund S. Morgan and Helen M. Morgan, *The Stamp Act Crisis* (Chapel Hill: University of North Carolina Press, 1995), 8–9. Thomas Hutchinson, *The History of the Province of Massachusetts Bay*, vol. 3, ed. John Hutchinson (London: John Murray, 1828), 254. As far as buying one's commission, it's useful to know that it was in some ways more of a pay-to-play world then than now. One had to essentially buy his office in government or the military.

15. Bailyn, *Ordeal*, 46.

16. Cary, *Joseph Warren*, 36.

17. Quincy, *Reports*, 407–8.

18. Bailyn, *Ordeal*, 47.

19. Quincy, *Reports*, 410–11. Bailyn, *Ordeal*, 48–50.

20. Quincy, *Reports*, 401–2, 405–6.

21. Quincy, *Reports*, 412–14. John Adams, *Legal Papers*, 2:113.

22. John Adams, *Legal Papers*, 2:106.

23. Ibid., 2:125.

24. Ibid., 2:127.

25. Ibid., 2:128. With the restrictions of the Iron Act of 1750, colonists could ship ore back to England but were forbidden furnaces and forges of their own. "But," writes Edgard Moreno, "similar to other laws, the 'Iron Act' proved to be unenforceable and by 1770 the colonies had a greater number of forges and furnaces than England and Wales combined." Edgard Moreno, "Patriotism and Profit," in *Paul Revere: Artisan, Businessman, and Patriot* (Boston: Paul Revere Memorial Association, 1988), 97.

26. Said Coke, "When an act of Parliament is against common right and reason, or repugnant, or impossible to be performed, the common law will control it and adjudge such act to be void." For more: John Adams, *Legal Papers*, 2:117–22.

27. Harold J. Berman, *Law and Revolution II* (Cambridge: Harvard University Press, 2004), 245. The line goes all the way

back to Chaucer's *Parliament of Foules*: "Out of olde feldys as men sey / Comyth all this newe corn from yere to yere."

28. Quincy, *Reports*, 415.

7. Pox

1. Nielsen, "Revere Family," 299.
2. Skerry, "Revolutionary Revere," 47.
3. Ibid.
4. Ibid. David R. Brigham, "Paul Revere Silver."
5. Triber, *True Republican*, 37–38.
6. William Henry Whitmore et al., eds., *A Report of the Record Commissioners of the City of Boston, Containing the Selectmen's Minutes from 1764 Through 1768* (Boston: Rockwell and Churchill, 1889), 1, 8.
7. Harlow Giles Unger, *John Hancock* (New York: Wiley, 2000), 64. Whitmore, *Commissioners of Boston*, 18.
8. Unger, *John Hancock*, 64–65.
9. Triber, *True Republican*, 38.
10. Whitmore, *Commissioners of Boston*, 1, 3, 11.
11. Ibid., 6, 7, 15.
12. Ibid., 27.
13. Ibid., 31–32, 40–41. Forbes, *Paul Revere and the World*, 74.
14. Whitmore, *Commissioners of Boston*, 39–40.
15. Ibid., 44.
16. Forbes, *Paul Revere and the World*, 74–75.
17. Whitmore, *Commissioners of Boston*, 54.
18. Ibid., 57–58.
19. Nielsen, "Revere Family," 299.
20. Steblecki, *Paul Revere and Freemasonry*, 11.
21. Whitmore, *Commissioners of Boston*, 55. Steblecki, *Paul Revere and Freemasonry*, 12. Charles W. Moore, "The Green Dragon Tavern, or Freemasons' Arms," *The Builder*, August 1923.
22. Samuel Adams, *The Writings of Samuel Adams*, vol. 1, ed. Harry Alonzo Cushing (New York: Octagon, 1968), 5.
23. Jack P. Greene, ed., *Colonies to Nation* (New York: McGraw-Hill, 1967), 31.

8. RIOTS

1. Triber, *True Republican*, 38.
2. Brigham, *Paul Revere's Engravings*, 17.
3. Ibid., 18.
4. Goss, *Life of Colonel Paul Revere*, 1:54.
5. Triber, *True Republican*, 39.
6. Ibid., 40. Brigham, *Paul Revere's Engravings*, 18.
7. J. L. Bell, "A Bankruptcy in Boston, 1765," *Massachusetts Banker*, 4th quarter, 2008. Forbes, *Paul Revere and the World*, 95. Triber, *True Republican*, 38. As Bell details the magnitude of this quake, Wheelwright's debts were more than 60 percent "of all the goods traded between Britain and New England in 1762."
8. Benjamin L. Carp, *Rebels Rising* (New York: Oxford University Press, 2007), 38.
9. Russell Bourne, *Cradle of Violence* (New York: Wiley, 2006), 96.
10. Brigham, *Paul Revere's Engravings*, 19–20.
11. Triber, *True Republican*, 41.
12. Nielsen, "Revere Family," 299.
13. Pauline Maier, *From Resistance to Revolution* (New York: Norton, 1991), 307.
14. Triber, *True Republican*, 45.
15. Riots such as this (and several others we'll soon see in Boston and Britain) were not uncommon. England had a long history of democracy by violence. In 1497, for instance, a Cornish army marched on London and battled the king's men at Blackheath to oppose high taxes. Rebellions such as this "had been a measure of the inability of the more rudimentary Parliament to act as a safety-valve for discontent," says historian J. A. Williamson. But even after Parliament improved following Elizabeth's ascension, it was never perfect, and people who felt unheard or disregarded sometimes forced regard by mob action. J. A. Williamson, *Great Britain and the Empire* (London: Adam and Charles Black, 1946), 30.
16. Morgan and Morgan, *The Stamp Act Crisis*, 131.

17. Ibid.
18. Bernard Bailyn, *Faces of Revolution* (New York: Vintage, 1992), 127.
19. Ibid. Akers, *Called unto Liberty*, 202–4.)
20. Quincy, *Reports*, 422.
21. Ibid.
22. Thomas Hutchinson, *History*, 124–25. Bailyn, *Ordeal*, 35–36.
23. Bailyn, *Faces*, 128.
24. Ibid., 127.
25. Quincy, *Reports*, 416.
26. Morgan and Morgan, *The Stamp Act Crisis*, 133
27. Forbes, *Paul Revere and the World*, 104. The Poor Richard line comes from Ben Franklin's essay, "The Way to Wealth."
28. Triber, *True Republican*, 49.

9. Parties

1. Nielsen, "Revere Family," 299.
2. Steblecki, *Paul Revere and Freemasonry*, 1–2, 20–21.
3. Goss, *Life of Colonel Paul Revere*, 1:35–36. Gettemy, *True Story of Paul Revere*, 11.
4. Goss, *Life of Colonel Paul Revere*, 1:39–46. Gettemy, *True Story of Paul Revere*, 12–16.
5. [Benjamin Bussey Thatcher], *Traits of the Tea Party* (New York: Harper, 1835), 72. Name is in brackets because author is unknown; Thatcher is commonly thought to be the author. Brigham, *Paul Revere's Engravings*, 26. Goss, *Life of Colonel Paul Revere*, 1:36. Forbes, *Paul Revere and the World*, 111.
6. Brigham, *Paul Revere's Engravings*, 26.
7. Thatcher, *Traits of the Tea Party*, 72–74. Brigham, *Paul Revere's Engravings*, 27. Forbes, *Paul Revere and the World*, 111–112.
8. For a full account of the plate, see Brigham, *Paul Revere's Engravings*, 26–31.
9. Ellis Sandoz, ed., *Political Sermons of the American Founding Era* (Indianapolis: Liberty Fund, 1990), 244, 260, 262–63.
10. Triber, *True Republican*, 55.

11. Bradford, *Rev. Jonathan Mayhew*, 429. Akers, *Called unto Liberty*, 218.

12. Akers, *Called unto Liberty*, 218–19.

13. Bradford, *Rev. Jonathan Mayhew*, 430–31. Akers, *Called unto Liberty*, 220.

14. John Rowe, *The Diary of John Rowe* (Cambridge: John Wilson and Son, 1895), 27.

15. Brigham, *Paul Revere's Engravings*, 32–35.

16. Jeffrey B. Walker, *The Devil Undone* (New York: Arno, 1982), 67–68.

17. Sandoz, *Political Sermons*, 264.

18. Zobel, *Boston Massacre*, 50.

10. Boycotts

1. Brigham, *Paul Revere's Engravings*, 36–38.

2. Triber, *True Republican*, 74, 56. Zobel, *Boston Massacre*, 51.

3. Triber, *True Republican*, 57. Zobel, *Boston Massacre*, 55.

4. Zobel, *Boston Massacre*, 52.

5. Ibid., 54–55.

6. Samuel Adams, *Writings*, 1:96.

7. Warden, *Boston*, 182–83.

8. Zobel, *Boston Massacre*, 65.

9. Ibid., 62.

10. Ibid., 64.

11. T. H. Breen, *The Marketplace of Revolution* (New York: Oxford University Press, 2004), 240–41.

12. Ibid., 236.

13. Richard Frothingham, *Life and Times of Joseph Warren* (Boston: Little, Brown, 1865), 38–39.

14. Zobel, *Boston Massacre*, 65. Bourne, *Cradle of Violence*, 135.

15. Frothingham, *Warren*, 32.

16. Zobel, *Boston Massacre*, 69.

17. Samuel Adams, *Writings*, 1:184.

18. Ibid., 1:185–86.

19. Ibid., 1:188.

20. Zobel, *Boston Massacre*, 71.

21. Ibid., 71. Warden, *Boston*, 188.

22. Warden, *Boston*, 186, 360.

23. Zobel, *Boston Massacre*, 70.

24. Nielsen, "Revere Family," 300.

25. Ibid., 300. Forbes, *Paul Revere and the World*, 113, 166.

26. Samuel Adams Drake, *Old Landmarks and Historic Personages of Boston* (Boston: James R. Osgood, 1873), 161.

27. Akers, *Called unto Liberty*, 224.

28. Triber, *True Republican*, 216.

29. Brigham, *Paul Revere's Engravings*, 211. Zobel, *Boston Massacre*, 67.

30. Brigham, *Paul Revere's Engravings*, 211.

31. Goss, *The Life of Colonel Paul Revere*, 2:440–44. People took close note of teeth in Paul's day. Dr. Benjamin Church once mauled celebrated Harvard tutor Henry Flynt in verse by focusing on his maw: "His Face a mixture of Deformities, / Like flaming meteors, shine his Gorgon Eyes. / A very Scarecrow is his awful Nose. / A frightful Grin his hideous Jaws disclose; / You'll, when he yawns, tremendous teeth may see, / And hence he's call'd his Dental Majesty." See Walker, *The Devil Undone*, 133–34.

32. Goss, *Life of Colonel Paul Revere*, 2:446. Forbes, *Paul Revere and the World*, 107.

33. Forbes, *Paul Revere and the World*, 107–10. Jonathan Fairbanks et al. *Paul Revere's Boston* (Boston: Museum of Fine Arts, 1975), 18–19.

34. Fairbanks, *Paul Revere's Boston*, 124–25.

35. Zobel, *Boston Massacre*, 74.

36. Unger, *John Hancock*, 120.

37. Zobel, *Boston Massacre*, 75–76. Warden, *Boston*, 192.

11. Showdown

1. Bailyn, *Ordeal*, 121.

2. Brigham, *Paul Revere's Engravings*, 43–47. Goss, *Life of Colonel Paul Revere*, 1:58–62. Forbes, *Paul Revere and the World*, 129. As with earlier etchings, Revere here

portrayed a complicated political struggle in a simple image that separated the sheep from the goats and gave his audience a clear target for their outrage. But he wasn't usually original. He very often copied other people's designs to get his point across. The practice was common enough, and there wasn't much concern for intellectual property rights. But soon enough Revere nonetheless landed himself in a pickle for pinching someone else's design.

3. Brigham, *Paul Revere's Engravings*, 43–47. Goss, *Life of Colonel Paul Revere*, 1:58–62. Forbes, *Paul Revere and the World*, 129–30.

4. Goss, *Life of Colonel Paul Revere*, 1:62.

5. Brigham, *Paul Revere's Engravings*, 46.

6. Fairbanks, *Paul Revere's Boston*, 118–19. Goss, *Life of Colonel Paul Revere*, 1:62–65. Warden, *Boston*, 216.

7. John Wilkes, *The North Briton*, vol. 1 (London: John Mitchell and James Williams, 1766), 261–69.

8. Arthur H. Cash, *John Wilkes* (New Haven: Yale University Press, 2007), 232.

9. Ibid., 221, 223.

10. Zobel, *Boston Massacre*, 83.

11. Warden, *Boston*, 194.

12. Brigham, *Paul Revere's Engravings*, 79.

13. Triber, *True Republican*, 66. Thomas Hutchinson, *History*, 225.

14. Steblecki, *Paul Revere and Freemasonry*, 20–21.

15. Brigham, *Paul Revere's Engravings*, 49–51.

16. Jack P. Greene, ed., *Colonies to Nation* (New York: McGraw-Hill, 1967), 161.

17. Ibid., 162.

18. Ibid., 163, emphasis in the original.

19. Bailyn, *Ordeal*, 128–30.

20. Thomas Hutchinson, *History*, 226–27. Samuel Adams, *Writings*, 1:334.

21. Rowe, *Diary*, 71. Zobel, *Boston Massacre*, 111.

22. Thomas Hutchinson, *History*, 225, 238. Zobel, *Boston Massacre*, 112, 335.

23. Samuel Adams, *Writings*, 1:339–40, emphasis in the original.

24. Thomas Hutchinson, *History*, 239.

25. Samuel Adams, *Writings*, 1:349–54.

26. Thomas Hutchinson, *History*, 238.

27. Ibid., 241. Zobel, *Boston Massacre*, 132.

28. Zobel, *Boston Massacre*, 132–33.

29. Thomas Hutchinson, *History*, 254. Rowe, *Diary*, 72. Zobel, *Boston Massacre*, 133–34.

12. Skirmishes

1. *Boston Gazette*, 21 August 1769. See also Ellen Chase, *The Beginnings of the American Revolution*, vol. 1 (New York: Baker and Taylor, 1910), 132–33.

2. *Boston Gazette*, 21 August 1769. John Adams, *Works*, 2:218.

3. "Focus on: The Sons of Liberty," *From Our Cabinet*, Massachusetts Historical Society, August 2001, http://www.masshist.org/cabinet/august2001/august2001.html.

4. *Boston Gazette*, 21 August 1769, quotes at length at http://www.oneapril.com/sons/fortyfivetoasts.shtml

5. John Adams, *Works*, 2:218.

6. Francis Samuel Drake, *The Town of Roxbury* (Boston: Municipal Printing Office, 1908), 166.

7. John Adams, *Works*, 2:218. Rowe, *Diary*, 72.

8. Ellis Gray, "Father of the Revolution," *Harper's New Monthly Magazine*, vol. LIII, June–November, 1876 (New York: Harper, 1876), 191.

9. John Adams, *Works*, 2:219. *Boston Gazette*, 4 September 1769, as reproduced in Armand Francis Lucier, *Boston, the Redcoats, and the Homespun Patriots* (Bowie, MD: Heritage Books, 1998), 165. William Tudor, *The Life of James Otis of Massachusetts* (Boston: Wells and Lilly, 1823), 360–62.

10. Zobel, *Boston Massacre*, 148. *Boston Gazette*, 11 September 1769, as reproduced in Lucier, *Boston, the Redcoats*, 166–67. Tudor, *Life of James Otis*, 362–63.

11. Chase, *Beginnings of the American Revolution*, 1:135.

12. Zobel, *Boston Massacre*, 148–49. *Boston Gazette*, 11 September 1769, as reproduced in Lucier, *Boston, the Redcoats*, 167.

13. Rowe, *Diary*, 72.
14. Unger, *John Hancock*, 136. Zobel, *Boston Massacre*, 154.
15. Zobel, *Boston Massacre*, 156–58, 162–63. Thomas Hutchinson, *History*, 259–60. Unger, *John Hancock*, 137.
16. Warden, *Boston*, 366.
17. Triber, *True Republican*, 66–67.
18. Kathryn C. Buhler, *Paul Revere, Goldsmith* (Boston: Museum of Fine Arts, n.d.), items 10, 11, 29, and 44.
19. Steblecki, *Paul Revere and Freemasonry*, 19, 21–22.
20. Even to this day, while the organization is far from orthodox, Masons claim John the Evangelist and John the Baptist as patron saints. From the earliest days of the group, they, like the rest of Western Christendom, observed their respective feast days: 27 December and 24 June. Jasper Ridley, *The Freemasons* (New York: Arcade, 2001), 9.
21. Frothingham, *Warren*, 115–16.
22. Goss, *Life of Colonel Paul Revere*, 1:26. Forbes, *Paul Revere and the World*, 162. Triber, *True Republican*, 71.
23. Nielsen, "Revere Family," 298–300.
24. Forbes, *Paul Revere and the World*, 165.
25. Triber, *True Republican*, 74. Thomas Hutchinson, *History*, 269. Zobel, *Boston Massacre*, 174–75. Thomas J. Fleming, "Verdicts of History 1: The Boston Massacre," *American Heritage*, December 1966.
26. Zobel, *Boston Massacre*, 175. Most of Richardson's pellets hit Christopher Seider in his chest and abdomen.

13. MASSACRE

1. Thatcher, *Traits of the Tea Party*, 93, emphasis in the original.
2. Thomas Hutchinson, *History*, 269–70. Triber, *True Republican*, 75. Maier, *From Resistance to Revolution*, 194.
3. Zobel, *Boston Massacre*, 182. Fleming, "Verdicts." Triber, *True Republican*, 75.
4. Zobel, *Boston Massacre*, 182–83. Thatcher, *Traits of the Tea Party*, 97–98. Triber, *True Republican*, 75–76. Frothingham, *Warren*, 121–22. Bourne, *Cradle of Violence*, 155.

5. Frothingham, *Warren*, 123.
6. Ibid., 124–25.
7. Ibid., 126.
8. [James Hawkes], *A Retrospect of the Boston Tea-Party* (New York: S. S. Bliss, 1834), 28–29. Name is in brackets because the author is unknown. Thatcher, *Traits of the Tea Party*, 103–4. Frothingham, *Warren*, 126. Because of their red coats, *lobster* and *lobsterback* were common insults for British soldiers stationed in Boston.
9. Drake, *Old Landmarks*, 71. Zobel, *Boston Massacre*, 192–94. Fleming, "Verdicts."
10. Zobel, *Boston Massacre*, 195. Drake, *Old Landmarks*, 85. Also see Noah Brooks, *Henry Knox* (Cranbury: Scholar's Bookshelf, 2005), 8.
11. Fleming, "Verdicts." Zobel, *Boston Massacre*, 194–95.
12. Miller, *Origins of the American Revolution*, 296.
13. Ibid., 296. Zobel, *Boston Massacre*, 195. I've slightly altered the quotes as given here for effect.
14. Miller, *Origins of the American Revolution*, 297.
15. Thatcher, *Traits of the Tea Party*, 113–14.
16. Brigham, *Paul Revere's Engravings*, 62, 199.
17. Zobel, Goss, *Life of Colonel Paul Revere*, 1:72–75. *Boston Massacre*, 211.
18. Brigham, *Paul Revere's Engravings*, 62, 199.
19. Ibid., 52–78.
20. Ibid., 79.
21. Ibid., 86–92. Goss, *Life of Colonel Paul Revere*, 1:54–58.

14. Ebb

1. Triber, *True Republican*, 85.
2. Ibid., 85. Forbes, *Paul Revere and the World*, 172–73.
3. Unger, *John Hancock*, 154. Triber, *True Republican*, 84.
4. Thomas Hutchinson, *History*, 347.
5. Unger, *John Hancock*, 157–58.
6. Goss, *Life of Colonel Paul Revere*, vol. 2, appendix C.
7. Steblecki, *Paul Revere and Freemasonry*, 103.
8. Ibid., 24. Moore, "The Green Dragon Tavern."

9. Maier, *From Resistance to Revolution*, 208. Bailyn, *Ordeal*, 194.

10. Triber, *True Republican*, 88.

11. Ibid., 87.

12. Miller, *Origins of the American Revolution*, 325ff.

13. Ibid., 329.

14. Forbes, *Paul Revere and the World*, 174.

15. Steblecki, *Paul Revere and Freemasonry*, 11–14.

16. Triber, *True Republican*, 90.

17. Labaree, *Boston Tea Party*, 58–74, 88.

18. Frothingham, *Warren*, 228.

19. Goss, *Life of Colonel Paul Revere*, 1:110.

15. Flow

1. Triber, *True Republican*, 91.

2. Ibid., 90. Steblecki, *Paul Revere and Freemasonry*, 13–14.

3. Triber, *True Republican*, 91, 226. Forbes, *Paul Revere and the World*, 176. Charles Ferris Gettemy, *The True Story of Paul Revere* (Boston: Little, Brown, 1905), 36.

4. Rowe, *Diary*, 79.

5. Forbes, *Paul Revere and the World*, 163.

6. Goss, *Life of Colonel Paul Revere*, 1:110.

7. Forbes, *Paul Revere and the World*, 178.

8. Goss, *Life of Colonel Paul Revere*, 1:111.

9. Bailyn, *Ordeal*, 227–28. Thomas Hutchinson, *History*, 223–28. Miller, *Origins of the American Revolution*, 330.

10. Triber, *True Republican*, 91.

11. Labaree, *Boston Tea Party*, 88.

12. Ibid., 77.

13. Ibid., 79.

14. Goss, *Life of Colonel Paul Revere*, vol. 2, appendix C.

15. Maier, *From Resistance to Revolution*, 213.

16. Goss, *Life of Colonel Paul Revere*, 1:119–21.

17. Ibid., 1:121.

18. Gettemy, *True Story of Paul Revere*, 46–48. Labaree, *Boston Tea Party*, 137.

19. Labaree, *Boston Tea Party*, 138.

20. Triber, *True Republican*, 95.
21. Labaree, *Boston Tea Party*, 139–41.
22. Goss, *Life of Colonel Paul Revere*, 1:127.
23. Labaree, *Boston Tea Party*, 141. Goss, *Life of Colonel Paul Revere*, 1:127–28. Fischer, *Paul Revere's Ride*, 25. Nielsen, "Revere Family," 304.
24. Samuel Adams, *Writings*, 1:72–73. Goss, *Life of Colonel Paul Revere*, 1:132.
25. Gettemy, *True Story of Paul Revere*, 51.

16. EXPRESS

1. Forbes, *Paul Revere and the World*, 199.
2. Gettemy, *True Story of Paul Revere*, 52. Thomas Hutchinson, *History*, 441.
3. Triber, *True Republican*, 95.
4. Goss, *Life of Colonel Paul Revere*, 1:128. Francis Samuel Drake, *Tea Leaves* (Boston: A. O. Crane, 1884), clxxvi.
5. Gettemy, *True Story of Paul Revere*, 52–53.
6. Triber, *True Republican*, 96. Brigham, *Paul Revere's Engravings*, 106–36.
7. Brigham, *Paul Revere's Engravings*, 102–5.
8. Ibid., 104.
9. Walker, *Devil Undone*, 93–94.
10. Goss, *Life of Colonel Paul Revere*, 1:136–37.
11. Ibid., 1:137.
12. Peter Hutchinson, *Thomas Hutchinson*, 100.
13. Goss, *Life of Colonel Paul Revere*, 1:148. Gettemy, *True Story of Paul Revere*, 56. Triber, *True Republican*, 98.
14. Goss, *Life of Colonel Paul Revere*, 1:149.
15. Ibid., 1:148.
16. Ibid., 1:148–49. Gettemy, *True Story of Paul Revere*, 58–59.
17. Goss, *Life of Colonel Paul Revere*, 1:146.
18. Gettemy, *True Story of Paul Revere*, 57–58. Triber, *True Republican*, 98.
19. Chase, *Beginnings of the American Revolution*, 1:366. Triber, *True Republican*, 98.
20. Ray Raphael, *The First American Revolution* (New York: New Press, 2002), 48.

21. Goss, *Life of Colonel Paul Revere*, 1:151.
22. Fischer, *Paul Revere's Ride*, 41. Raphael, *First American Revolution*, 48–49, 53.
23. Fischer, *Paul Revere's Ride*, 42.
24. Triber, *True Republican*, 99.
25. Raphael, *First American Revolution*, 109–10. Triber, *True Republican*, 99.
26. Raphael, *First American Revolution*, 112–13. Fischer, *Paul Revere's Ride*, 44–45.
27. Goss, *Life of Colonel Paul Revere*, 1:150. Gettemy, *True Story of Paul Revere*, 60.
28. Raphael, *First American Revolution*, 150–51. Frothingham, *Warren*, 529.
29. Goss, *Life of Colonel Paul Revere*, 1:161.
30. Ibid., 1:169.
31. Revere, *Three Accounts of Ride*, third account.
32. Ibid.
33. Gettemy, *True Story of Paul Revere*, 165–66.
34. Fischer, *Paul Revere's Ride*, 31, 87.
35. Triber, *True Republican*, 101.
36. Gettemy, *True Story of Paul Revere*, 129.

17. Ride!

1. Triber, *True Republican*, 95–96.
2. Robert A. Gross, *The Minutemen and Their World* (New York: Hill and Wang, 1989), 112–14.
3. Revere, *Three Accounts of Ride*, third account. Fischer, *Paul Revere's Ride*, 86–87.
4. Goss, *Life of Colonel Paul Revere*, 1:229–30.
5. Fischer, *Paul Revere's Ride*, 87.
6. Triber, *True Republican*, 102. Gross, *Minutemen and Their World*, 113.
7. Revere, *Three Accounts of Ride*, third account. Fischer, *Paul Revere's Ride*, 88. Gross, *Minutemen and Their World*, 114.
8. Gross, *Minutemen and Their World*, 113.
9. Revere, *Three Accounts of Ride*, third account. Fischer, *Paul Revere's Ride*, 88.

10. Goss, *Life of Colonel Paul Revere*, 1:248.
11. Fischer details several of these rumors and reports, *Paul Revere's Ride*, 93–95.
12. Fischer, *Paul Revere's Ride*, 95–97, 387n14. To this day the identity of Warren's Deep Throat remains clouded, but circumstantial evidence points to General Gage's own American-born and deeply conflicted wife, Margaret Kemble Gage. Goss presents this idea as a given in his treatment. Not all agree, however. Gettemy, for instance, reacts harshly against the notion, and Esther Forbes dismisses it as "gossip." But Fischer's take is, I think, convincing despite naysayers. Goss, *Life of Colonel Paul Revere*, 1:234–35. Gettemy, *True Story of Paul Revere*, 82–93. Forbes, *Paul Revere and the World*, 243.
13. Fischer, *Paul Revere's Ride*, 99–100, 103. Revere, *Three Accounts of Ride*, third account.
14. Fischer, *Paul Revere's Ride*, 103. Revere, *Three Accounts of Ride*, third account.
15. Fischer, *Paul Revere's Ride*, 104–5.
16. Revere, *Three Accounts of Ride*, third account.
17. Forbes, *Paul Revere and the World*, 247–48.
18. Revere, *Three Accounts of Ride*, first, second, and third accounts. Fischer, *Paul Revere's Ride*, 105–6. George F. Scheer and Hugh F. Rankin, *Rebels and Redcoats* (New York: Da Capo, 1957), 20.
19. Gettemy, *True Story of Paul Revere*, 104. Goss, *Life of Colonel Paul Revere*, 1:196, 199. Fischer, *Paul Revere's Ride*, 109–10. Forbes, *Paul Revere and the World*, 250.
20. Goss, *Life of Colonel Paul Revere*, 1:199. Fischer, *Paul Revere's Ride*, 110. Forbes, *Paul Revere and the World*, 250.
21. Revere, *Three Accounts of Ride*, third account. Fischer, *Paul Revere's Ride*, 110–11, 143.
22. Revere, *Three Accounts of Ride*, first, second, and third accounts.
23. Ibid., first, second, and third accounts.
24. Ibid., second account.
25. Ibid., second account.
26. Ibid., third account.

27. Henry W. Holland, *William Dawes and His Ride with Paul Revere* (Boston: John Wilson and Son, 1878), 37. Goss, *Life of Colonel Paul Revere*, 2:670.
28. Revere, *Three Accounts of Ride*, third account.
29. Ibid., third account.
30. Ibid., third account.
31. Ibid., first, second, and third accounts.
32. Ibid., first and second accounts.
33. Ibid., first account.
34. Ibid., first, second, and third accounts.
35. Ibid., first, second, and third accounts.
36. Ibid., first, second, and third accounts.
37. Ibid., third account.

18. Betrayal

1. Revere, *Three Accounts of Ride*, third account.
2. Gettemy, *True Story of Paul Revere*, 122. Forbes, *Paul Revere and the World*, 266. Paul had billed for five shillings a day but the amount was reduced.
3. Revere, *Three Accounts of Ride*, third account.
4. The depositions were part of a public relations effort by the patriots to get their side of the story out in front of the world. See Triber, *True Republican*, 111, and Fischer, *Paul Revere's Ride*, 273–80. Revere's first and second accounts were produced during these sessions.
5. Revere, *Three Accounts of Ride*, third account.
6. Forbes, *Paul Revere and the World*, 266–67.
7. Revere, *Three Accounts of Ride*, third account.
8. Triber, *True Republican*, 112–14.
9. Gettemy, *True Story of Paul Revere*, 127.
10. Ibid., 127–28.
11. Triber, *True Republican*, 115.
12. Forbes, *Paul Revere and the World*, 270.
13. Walker, *Devil Undone*, 98.
14. Brigham, *Paul Revere's Engravings*, 213–17. Gettemy, *True Story of Paul Revere*, 136–38.
15. Frothingham, *Warren*, 508–20, 546. Triber, *True Republican*, 116–18.

16. James Warren, *Warren-Adams Letters*, vol. 1 (Boston: Massachusetts Historical Society, 1917), 121. Douglas Southall Freeman, *Washington* (New York: Touchstone, 1995), 239–40. Walker, *Devil Undone*, 102–4.

17. Walker, *Devil Undone*, 81. Church seems to have been not so much swayed by ideological concerns as simply not wanting to end up with the short end of the stick. Writes Walker, "It is this concern for being on the winning side that best explains Church's later defection. Never as concerned with ideological differences between Tories [loyalists] and Whigs [patriots] as he was with the financial, social, and political advantages he might gain as one of the victors in the struggle, his decisions were always made with his own welfare in mind" (85). More on this point: p. 99.

18. Revere, *Three Accounts of Ride*, third account. Gross, *Minute Men and Their World*, 112–13.

19. Revere, *Three Accounts of Ride*, third account.

20. Walker, *Devil Undone*, 103.

19. Waiting

1. Brigham, *Paul Revere's Engravings*, 123.

2. Jack Kelly, *Gunpowder* (New York: Basic Books), 36, 161–62. Goss, *Life of Colonel Paul Revere*, 2:400–402.

3. Gettemy, *True Story of Paul Revere*, 168, 170–71. Goss, *Life of Colonel Paul Revere*, 2:403–4.

4. Samuel Adams, *The Writings of Samuel Adams*, vol. 3, ed. Harry Alonzo Cushing (New York: Octagon, 1968), 248. Goss, *Life of Colonel Paul Revere*, 2:404–5.

5. Gettemy, *True Story of Paul Revere*, 171.

6. Triber, *True Republican*, 123.

7. Frothingham, *Warren*, 522. Goss, *Life of Colonel Paul Revere*, 2:439.

8. Frothingham, *Warren*, 524.

9. Gettemy, *True Story of Paul Revere*, 147.

10. Triber, *True Republican*, 124. Goss, *Life of Colonel Paul Revere*, 1:277–78.

11. Nielsen, "Revere Family," 301. Triber, *True Republican*, 124–25.

12. Triber, *True Republican*, 126.
13. Bernard A. Weisberger, "Paul Revere," *American Heritage*, April 1977. Goss, *Life of Colonel Paul Revere*, 2:406. Triber, *True Republican*, 127, 242.
14. Ibid., 134.
15. Goss, *Life of Colonel Paul Revere*, 1:280.
16. Samuel Adams, *Writings*, 3:393–94.
17. Gettemy, *True Story of Paul Revere*, 152–55.
18. Ibid., 157.
19. George E. Buker, *The Penobscot Expedition* (Annapolis: Naval Institute Press, 2002), 5–9, 11.
20. Goss, *Life of Colonel Paul Revere*, 2:325–26.

20. Penobscot

1. George E. Buker, *The Penobscot Expedition* (Annapolis: Naval Institute Press, 2002), 29, 31.
2. Goss, *Life of Colonel Paul Revere*, 2:343–44.
3. Buker, *Penobscot Expedition*, 24.
4. Ibid., 26.
5. "18-pounder Revolutionary War Cannon," Fort Moultrie, National Park Service, 30 September 2005, http://www. nps.gov/fosu/planyourvisit/upload/18_Pounder_Cannon.pdf.
6. Jeff Kinard, *Artillery* (Santa Barbara: ABC-CLIO, 2007), 99. And there are those Dutch again. The *houwitser* was a seventeenth-century invention of Holland's enterprising artillerists.
7. Buker, *Penobscot Expedition*, 26.
8. Ibid., 25–26.
9. Ibid., 26.
10. Goss, *Life of Colonel Paul Revere*, 2:364. All references in Goss, 2:364–76, are to Revere's diary of the Penobscot campaign, which Goss reproduces.
11. Ibid., 2:364.
12. Buker, *Penobscot Expedition*, 34–35. C. B. Kevitt, *General Solomon Lovell and the Penobscot Expedition* (Weymouth: Self-Published, 1976), 3.
13. Buker, *Penobscot Expedition*, 36–38. Goss, *Life of Colonel*

Paul Revere, 2:364. Kevitt, *Lovell and the Penobscot Expedition*, 32. Kevitt references from pages 32–50 are to Lovell's diary of the Penobscot campaign, which Kevitt reproduces.

14. Goss, *Life of Colonel Paul Revere*, 2:364–67. Russell Bourne, "The Penobscot Fiasco," *American Heritage*, October 1974.

15. Goss, *Life of Colonel Paul Revere*, 2:367. Kevitt, *Lovell and the Penobscot Expedition*, 33. Buker, *Penobscot Expedition*, 39–40. Bourne, "Penobscot Fiasco."

16. Goss, *Life of Colonel Paul Revere*, 2:367. Buker, *Penobscot Expedition*, 41.

17. Buker, *Penobscot Expedition*, 42.

18. Kevitt, *Lovell and the Penobscot Expedition*, 4, 35. Buker, *Penobscot Expedition*, 43, 44. Bourne, "Penobscot Fiasco."

19. Goss, *Life of Colonel Paul Revere*, 2:367. Bourne, "Penobscot Fiasco." Buker, *Penobscot Expedition*, 47.

20. Buker, *Penobscot Expedition*, 44.

21. Goss, *Life of Colonel Paul Revere*, 2:367–68.

22. Ibid., 2:368–69. Kevitt, *Lovell and the Penobscot Expedition*, 35.

23. Goss, *Life of Colonel Paul Revere*, 2:369. Buker, *Penobscot Expedition*, 48.

24. Goss, *Life of Colonel Paul Revere*, 2:369. Kevitt, *Lovell and the Penobscot Expedition*, 38.

25. Goss, *Life of Colonel Paul Revere*, 2:369. Buker, *Penobscot Expedition*, 45–47, 53. Bourne, "Penobscot Fiasco."

26. Goss, *Life of Colonel Paul Revere*, 2:370–71. Kevitt, *Lovell and the Penobscot Expedition*, 39–47. Buker, *Penobscot Expedition*, 50–68.

27. Goss, *Life of Colonel Paul Revere*, 2:372. Kevitt, *Lovell and the Penobscot Expedition*, 46–47.

28. Goss, *Life of Colonel Paul Revere*, 2:372.

29. Ibid., 2:373. Kevitt, *Lovell and the Penobscot Expedition*, 48. Buker, *Penobscot Expedition*, 73.

30. Goss, *Life of Colonel Paul Revere*, 2:373–74.

31. Ibid., 2:352–353, 374–75. Kevitt, *Lovell and the Penobscot Expedition*, 50.

32. Goss, *Life of Colonel Paul Revere*, 2:376.

33. Buker, *Penobscot Expedition*, 132–33.
34. Ibid., 142.
35. Ibid., 148. Forbes, *Paul Revere and the World*, 346.
36. Triber, *True Republican*, 139.

21. FOUNDING

1. Buhler, *Paul Revere, Goldsmith*, item 31. Skerry, "Revolutionary Revere," 52. David R. Brigham, "Paul Revere Silver."
2. Gordon S. Wood, *The Radicalism of the American Revolution* (New York: Vintage, 1993), 232.
3. Deborah A. Federhen, "From Artisan to Entrepreneur," in *Paul Revere: Artisan, Businessman, and Patriot* (Boston: Paul Revere Memorial Association, 1988), 69.
4. Ibid., 84.
5. Goss, *Life of Colonel Paul Revere*, 2:527–28. Forbes, *Paul Revere and the World*, 357. Leehey, "Reconstructing Paul Revere," 30.
6. Federhen, "From Artisan to Entrepreneur," 83.
7. Ibid., 77.
8. Ibid., 77, 80–81.
9. Ibid., 80–81, 85.
10. Moreno, "Patriotism and Profit," 99.
11. Daniel Webster, *Speeches and Forensic Arguments*, vol. 2 (Boston: Perkins and Marvin, 1839), 225. Webster told this story in 1833.
12. Ibid., 225.
13. Arthur H. Nichols, "The Bells of Paul and Joseph W. Revere," in *Essex Institute Historical Collections*, vol. 47 (Salem: Essex Institute, 1911), 293.
14. Ibid., 294–95, 298, 302. Bernard A. Weisberger, "Paul Revere," *American Heritage*, April 1977.
15. Moreno, "Patriotism and Profit," 99.
16. Goss, *Life of Colonel Paul Revere*, 2:547.
17. Quincy, *Municipal History*, 17, 25, 40.
18. Goss, *Life of Colonel Paul Revere*, 2:483–84.

19. Goss, *Life of Colonel Paul Revere*, 2:583–86. Gettemy, *True Story of Paul Revere*, 265–68.

20. Goss, *Life of Colonel Paul Revere*, 2:590.

21. Ibid., 2:589.

22. Ibid., 2:541–43.

23. Ibid., 2:544.

24. Ibid., 2:548.

25. Ibid., 2:554–55.

26. Moreno, "Patriotism and Profit," 100.

27. Ibid., 100–102.

28. Darren Staloff, *Hamilton, Adams, Jefferson* (New York: Hill and Wang, 2005), 347.

29. Moreno, "Patriotism and Profit," 110.

30. Ibid., 112. Goss, *Life of Colonel Paul Revere*, 2:571–73. Weisberger, "Paul Revere." John Steele Gordon, *An Empire of Wealth* (New York: Harper, 2004), 136–37.

22. DEPARTURES

1. Forbes, *Paul Revere and the World*, 417–19. For readability, in the excerpts here I have removed Revere's original underscores.

2. John Calvin, *Institutes of the Christian Religion*, 3.25.

3. Forbes, *Paul Revere and the World*, 433–34.

4. Triber, *True Republican*, 194.

5. Gettemy, *True Story of Paul Revere*, 276.

6. Forbes, *Paul Revere and the World*, 440–42.

7. Ibid., 446.

8. Gettemy, *True Story of Paul Revere*, 278.

Thanks

irst and foremost, my family: My wife, Megan, whose patience and care is outmeasured only by her kindness, love, and grace. My children, Fionn and Felicity, whose inquisitive minds bring me inestimable joy. My parents, particularly my dad, the English teacher, who one day brought home a copy of Esther Forbes's brilliant biography of Paul Revere and stoked my appreciation of the founding generation. And my sister, Abby Lockett, who always encourages with her critiques.

My team at Nelson: My editors, Kristen Parrish, Heather Skelton, and D. B. Kellogg, each of whom in their own way helped coax and bully this book into existence. There is no way I could have done it without you. Same for Alice Sullivan, Janene MacIvor, and Renee Chavez. My designer, Kristen Vasgaard, whose critical and creative faculties are matched only by her long-suffering. My dogged sales and marketing team: Rick Spruill, Heather McCulloch, Tom Knight, Rick Shear, Chris Long, David McGee, Doug

291

Miller, Dale Wilstermann, Kristi Henson, Curt Harding, and Jason Jones. And my seasoned production team: Rosie York, Debbie Eicholtz, and Casey Hooper, who bend creativity into narrow schedules like expert contortionists. Any success is yours.

I am also indebted to the scholars and writers (living and departed) who not only blazed the Revere trail but hacked it out of a tangled wilderness of obscurity in the first place: Elbridge Henry Goss, Charles Ferris Gettemy, Esther Forbes, Clarence S. Brigham, Jane Triber, David Hackett Fischer, Edith J. Steblecki, Patrick M. Leehey, Donald M. Nielsen, Janine Skerry, Edgard Moreno, and Deborah A. Federhen. I'd also like to express my gratitude for the work of Josiah Quincy, L. Kinvin Wroth, Hiller B. Zobel, and George E. Buker, without whom my understanding of the writs of assistance case, the Boston Massacre, and the Penobscot Expedition would have been sorely lacking. All mistakes are my own.

The Author

Joel J. Miller is the author of two previous books, *Bad Trip* and *Size Matters*. His shorter writing has been featured in, among other publications, the *American Spectator* and *Reason*. He lives in Nashville, Tennessee, with his wife, Megan, and two children, Fionn and Felicity.

More Revere. For more about this book and the life of Paul Revere visit joeljmiller.com/revere.

Connect with Joel. There are three easy ways to connect:

joeljmiller.com
facebook.com/joeljmiller
twitter.com/joeljmiller

Index

Act of Uniformity, 1
Acts of Trade and Navigation. *See* Navigation Acts
Adams, Charles, 49
Adams, John, 55, 124, 146, 153, 267
Adams, John Quincy, 248
Adams, Samuel: and correspondence, 66, 100–1, 109, 114–15, 143, 167, 175, 218; and his "circular letter," 100–2, 109; and his quarrel with Hutchinson, 47, 73; and the Boston Tea Party, 165, 167; and the Constitution, 245–46; and the "midnight ride," xiii–xiv, 198; and the powder mill, 214; and the Tea Act, 162, 165; as Boston Son of Liberty, 112, 124; as Harvard student, 16; as Mason, 44; as Patriot leader, 44, 100–2, 114–15, 124, 135–36, 165, 167, 181, 182, 186, 218; death, 256; motion to create a Committee of Correspondence, 153; orders (from London) for arrest, 187–89; political defeat, 151; political victory, 80; portraits, 106, *48*, 171; reaction to the Bernard depositions, 95–96; relation to John Adams, 55; resolution to the General Court for a Continental Congress, 177; response to the Sugar Act, 66; role in the Provincial Congress, 186–88
Age of Reason, 24
Albany (New York), 31
American Indians, 12, 30, 32, 83, 227, 263

American Revolution, xii, xiii, 49, 200, 207–8, 211, 213, 214–15, 217–36, 238: beginning, 200; end of war, 238
Anglican Church: and the Act of Uniformity, 1; Paul's attendance at, 21–23
Ansart, Lewis (Col.), 217
anti-Federalists (Republicans), 246, 252
apprenticeship, 5, 9–11, 18–20, 27, 28, 34, 41, 44, 249
Articles of Confederation, 245
"Artillerists at work," *231*
artillery: equipment of Paul's day, *228*
Attucks, Crispus, 139, 142, 143
Avery, John, 73

Bagaduce, 220, 227, 228, 231, 237, 239
Bagley, Jonathan (Col.), 32
Bailyn, Bernard, 52
Balch, Nathaniel, 125
bankruptcy, 69, 71, 72, 253
Bank's Island, 228–31
Barnard, Joseph, 62
bartering, 14–15
Battle at Lexington, xii, *199*–200
Bay Colony. *See* Massachusetts Bay Colony
Belknap, Jeremy (Rev.), xii–xiv
bell: first cast in Boston, 247
bellcasting, 247
bellringers' guild, 21–22
Bernard, Francis (governor): and Adams's circular letter, 109–10; and appointment of Hutchinson as chief